jones knowles ritchie is a specialist de~~~~ ~~~~cuses on branded packaging, working with clients big and sn~~~~ ~~~~and global to help build competitive advantage for household names. ~~~~ne fundamental principle that underpins all of their work is that, above all else, the brand comes first.

Silas Amos was a founder designer at jkr in 1990. He writes the daily Design Gazette blog and is now a creative director at the company, with a leaning towards content and strategy.

Rory Sutherland joined OgilvyOne (formely O&M Direct) on graduation from Cambridge in 1988. After a short spell as an account executive and planner Rory turned his hand to being a copywriter in the creative department. His clear skills as a creative person saw his career take off rapidly and he soon became the Executive Creative Director and now he is the Vice Chairman of Ogilvy Group UK. Rory is an active blogger, twitter, social networker, TED Talker and old fashioned writer and speaker on the subject of 360 degree branding for which he is most passionate. It is this that has gained him notoriety in the industry and lead to his appointment as the President of the IPA.

the blue lady's new look and other curiosities

A "jkr Design Gazette" anthology
by Silas Amos

With an introduction by
Rory Sutherland

Designed by Silas Amos & Alex Stewart
Cover Illustration by Miss Swanne

First published by Jones Knowles Ritchie Dec 2010.

ISBN 978-0-9567161-0-1.

Published by

jkr Brand First Books
128 Albert Street
London
NW1 7NE

Preface

Another year, another anthology from the jkr Design Gazette. Having posted every working day for two years, I will confess that after a while new work serves to confirm and harden prejudices, rather than open up radical departures of opinion. Perhaps design is subject to certain eternal verities. If so, I hope that I am at least providing fresh illustrations of certain timeless principles. The notes you hold have been loosely stitched together from posts that were originally written day-to-day in reaction to whatever design or marketing work caught my eye. The views are subjective and far from comprehensive, but stood back from now, I hope these individual fragments of the mosaic give at least some impression of where branding finds itself and where it might be going.

The longer essay that closes the book draws together several themes from the past year and asks why everything today feels a bit familiar. We are working in an era which is unique for its level of self-reference and lack of a defining progressive style. This offers challenges and opportunities which the smarter brands are grasping to afford themselves competitive advantage.

Perhaps we are culturally drawing breath, or conversely are living in a time that will retrospectively be branded an 'ism'.

Either way, as Stan Lee had it, "Excelsior!"

Silas Amos

contents

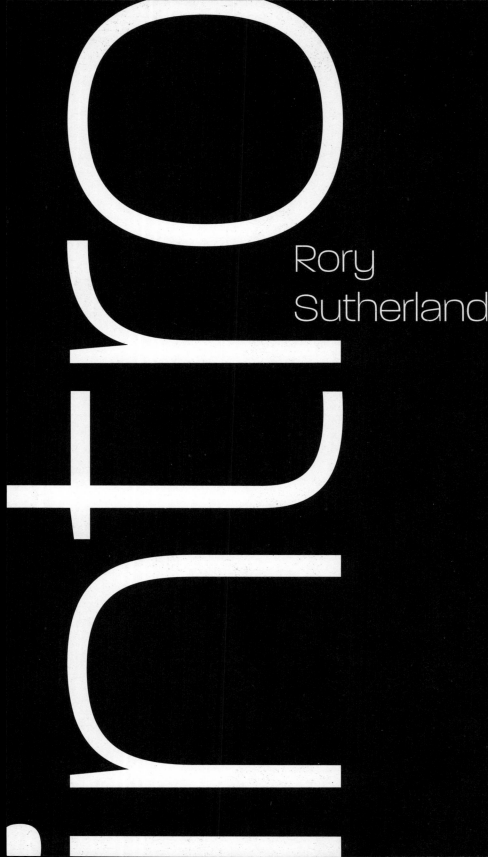

Rory
Sutherland

I have enjoyed reading this immensely.

At one level, it is a tremendously good anthology of some of the best and most ingenious marketing ideas of the last two years (and a few of the worst, too). It's valuable on its own simply for the author's encyclopaedic knowledge of marketing case lore.

But it also serves to make some really vital points.

The first is that, in marketing, generalisations are dangerous. I have always been a great fan of A. N. Whitehead's observation that "very often the opposite of a big idea is itself a big idea". Terminal 5 is a big idea... but so is London City Airport. Similarly making your logo enormous is a big idea; but making it invisible - or detectable only to a tiny few - is also a big idea.

As the author shows, good marketers need to be comfortable with ambiguity - with contradictions of this nature. Something which becomes more and more difficult as many of the levers of business decision-making rest in the hands of accountants and engineers - people for whom ambiguity arouses feelings of deep unease.

John Keats, writing about Shakepeare, described him as having a "negative capability". It was high praise. What impressed Keats was the fact that, while the playwright had an astounding capacity to understand and depict human behaviour and thinking, he never tried to force-fit his ideas into some rigid or all encompassing philosophical framework. Here was someone comfortable with complexity and ambiguity. And his real achievement lay in what he did not try to do - to simplify or to generalise or to eliminate contradictions.

The best ideas in this book are the work of people who share a little of this negative capability. The understanding that there are no hard and fast rules - and that almost nothing can be judged or understood without understanding its context. With these ideas comes the understanding that many of the most interesting brands contain an inherent contradiction - the ideas of 'invented nostaligia' and 'retro-progressive' in the final chapter are perfect examples of this.

But there is another contradiction in many of these ideas which also fascinates me. Many of them are big in their results but small in their execution. Great design often has what the Japanese call "shibumi" - the skill of achieving the greatest effects from the least intervention. Which means that the cost of great design can be remarkably modest - certainly compared to the value it adds to businesses and brands.

The problem this causes is that ironically, because great design is so inexpensive, it receives a fraction of the attention which it deserves within an organisation. Businesses now focus obsessively on cost cutting and financial engineering of large things, while the business of human-insight-led innovation, where real value is created, gets relatively little attention. The very cheese-paring approach which destroyed the British car industry is now being applied to almost everything else.

Yet the real question, where you ask how do you create more human value with fewer resources - a question which is pertinent to both the environmental movement and business in general - is not being answered enough.

Product design, experience design, framing, brand-value creation, intelligent R&D - all of these are the only sustainable ways to generate value with the lowest consumption of resources. Yet they are approached by business with the mentality that is applied to any other cost.

This is a tragedy.

If you doubt the value of this kind of intelligent, human focussed approach to business, one additional example should suffice.

Simply Google the phrase "The $300m button" by Jared M Spool.

It shows how a simple, insight-led change to an online retailer's check out page increased sales by $300m over the following twelve months.

How much were they paid for this insight, I wonder? If they were unlucky, probably a few days' worth of fees. Fees then negotiated down by the procurement department down the hallway.

Henry Ford didn't make this mistake. He was once asked by some efficiency consultants why he continued to pay a $100,000 salary to a man at the end of the corridor who seemed to do little more that "sit around with his feet on his desk".

"What you need to understand," said Henry, "was that a few years ago that man had an idea which made me $2m. And, when he had that idea, I seem to remember his feet were exactly where they are now."

distinctiveness

Media fragmentation, brand proliferation, a projected two billion computers worldwide by 2015 – our world is saturated in information and choice. Brands' evergreen need to cut distinctively through the noise and define what makes them unique amongst the flotsam and jetsam has never been more challenging, or more vital for their continued survival. Globalisation adds yet another dimension: witness for example, how Bolivia's Coca Colla brand puts that socialist nation's coca plant crop to legitimate use with familiarly capitalist red and white iconography. So it's timely to consider some of what can make a brand stand out and stand for something in our blink-and-you'd-miss-it world.

Style or substance, something has to hold the line

When author Tom Wolfe turned eighty, newspaper tributes made much of his 'trademark' white suit. One hopes his dry-cleaner sent him a nice birthday card: he's been modelling the outfit since 1962, augmenting the look over time with other props – spats, a cane, a hat. With his distinctive and rarely changing attire, Wolfe is amongst the few authors you might confidently recognise without ever having read a word he has written.

Wolfe claims the outfit disarms the people he observes, making him, in their eyes, "a man from Mars, the man who didn't know anything and was eager to know".[1]

But it's equally true that the outfit has helped make Wolfe the centre of his own stories and provides a visual shorthand for 'brand Wolfe'. It's become a feature of the book and magazine covers that help further boost his standing. Evidence perhaps that single-minded and repetitive consistency is much more effective than makeovers which revamp the image in pursuit of the zeitgeist.

But if you have a less arresting brand than Wolfe's the counterapproach – a limitless flow of variations on a theme – avoids the risk of typecasting. AOL's rebranding featured myriad images, from a goldfish to clouds of ink, framing the wordmark. Less corporate, more flexible and in tune with the smörgåsbord nature of the product offer. "Historically brand identity has been monolithic and controlling, little more than stamping a company name on a product. AOL is a 21st century media company, with an ambitious vision for the future and new focus on creativity and expression. This required the new brand identity to be open and generous, to invite conversation and collaboration and to feel credible, but also aspirational", explained the press release, laying it on a bit thick. Especially as Google has been taking this "variations on a theme" approach for years on their homepage.

Google was far from the first: for example, since 1937 there have been some 2,000 unique Hermès scarf designs – all different, all clearly part of the same family. Received wisdom has it that being consistent is effective... but also that refreshing brands is important. AOL, Hermès and Google offer proof perhaps that being regularly inconsistent can itself be the glue that holds a brand together. But in order to be visually eclectic you need the rock solid foundation of an unchanging product offer, which can be as limiting as having an unbending image. Conversely Tom Wolfe wrote and writes about anything and everything – but his distinctive unchanging image acts as an umbrella to his diverse product and a guarantee of the uniform excellence of his work.

The Armani ad as it appeared...

...and how one MP saw it.

Sex sells. But can it brand?

For as long as they've been wielding the paintbrush to sell things, men have placed alluring women at the heart of the story. The original lithographic posters of the late nineteenth century (which can be seen as the beginning of modern advertising) typically featured pretty girls, regardless of their relevance to the products being sold. Sex sells, obviously. More than a century later just putting a pretty face on a campaign might get it noticed, but won't necessarily guarantee it will be remembered for the right reasons.

When Conservative MP Nadine Dorries called for a ban on advertising featuring scantily clad women in public spaces she was concerned about the ads' corrosive effect on young girls' self-image. She was specifically riled by images of Megan Fox plastered on buses for Armani. Dorries noted that "on the Armani ads you can barely see the name of the company". Looking at the ad in question, clearly Dorries[2] is mistaken. But her perception is revealing if one is viewing the issue from the amoral perspective of effective branding: Fox's charms eclipsed the brand in Dorries' mind's eye. In truth, the generically sexy black and white photography could come from any number of brands and Dorries' perception reflects the interchangeable nature of such branding. In contrast, the equally sexy "Hello Boys" Wonderbra ad made that brand famous despite deploying a proportionally tiny logo. I think they achieved this by making the image and copy all about the product rather than the model. Clearly if you are going to use a nice pair of boobs to sell your product, it takes careful handling to ensure they don't overshadow the brand.

BBH made playful use of advertising's reliance on images of interchangeable scantily clad women in their tube adverts for Lynx Rise shower gel. As you ascend a tube escalator a sequence of beautiful girls hold their names on cards – ending with the question "What was the brunette called? (Because girls like it if you can remember stuff like their name)." A sly gag.

Perhaps it is photography, or at least the generic use of it, rather than the women themselves which makes such branding forgettable. Those old lithographs tended to stay in the mind as much for the idiosyncratic illustration styles of the artists as for the women they portrayed. All of which assumes we're okay with the idea of objectifying women in the first place – but that's a whole different debate...

If form follows function
where do you put the branding?

In 1896 American architect Louis Sullivan set out a design principle which informs much in our modern world: "form ever follows function". To which Adolf Loos, one father of modernism, added: "ornament is a crime".

It's all about balance. Form clearly plays an important part in branding (otherwise all cars would be identical products of wind tunnel physics). What does Google look like in your mind's eye? To me it's bright, white and primary-coloured – a kind of technological Benetton. Yet despite being a colourful brand in a techie world of monochromes, Google's first Nexus phone bypassed these equities opting for something more stylistically conventional (as a possible result of using off-the-peg styling provided by the manufacturer). The Nexus, some said, had product superiority over the iPhone but its familiar appearance made it feel less 'game-changing'. Perhaps Google aimed to make design a moot point, choosing to focus debate on product comparisons they could win rather than style comparisons they might lose? If so, there are many precedents where product superiority has failed against less able but more 'stylish' rivals. The Google Nexus was perhaps too focused on function at the expense of form to really be a hit.

But a transient over-reliance on function-free form can also backfire (hence all those obsolete domestic products which once seemed the last word in style but are now landfill). The best brands promote style and substance in equal measure. Dyson shows just how much distinctiveness can be achieved when form does justice to superior function. When Dyson took legal action against rival Vax, accusing the brand of copying one of Dyson's first bagless vacuums, Vax was adamant that its product was an evolution of the original design produced 15 years before. At issue was technical design not styling, but you could argue that the Vax styling so closely mirrors Dyson's that it can only feel like a pale imitation. In following its rival's visual gestalt Vax arguably gifted thought-leader Dyson the upper hand, whatever the legalities (Vax won the case). Effective branding comes through the balance of form and function, not the badging.

Dyson, meanwhile, doubled its profits in 2010, thanks to the success of its hand driers and bladeless fan. After misfires such as their stylish washing machine it appears that they have landed on their true equity – as expert shapers of air. Their products reform category norms and with design that has a symbiotic relationship between distinctive form and function, they don't even need a logo to tell you who they are.

Is gender bending ok for brands?

Brand extension tends to be about building on equities and selling broadly more to the same consumers. Overtly male or female brands that try to cross the gender divide do so in search of big new audiences, but they face a challenging leap. While society as a whole might be getting more relaxed about gender blurring, at point of purchase it seems we become throwbacks from less freewheeling, laissez-faire times. Put bluntly, most blokes wouldn't be caught dead buying into a 'girlie' brand. Women, typically, have fewer hang-ups about buying into archetypal masculine products.

It's not impossible to change a brand's gender: Marlboro, for example, was once a ladies' brand. With a lipstick-friendly red filter and the strapline "as mild as May", the all-white pack of the 1920s would have been out of place in your typical cowboy's saddlebag. A bold angular red chevron and a long-running campaign featuring real men (rather than models pretending to be real men) smoking in Stetsons and voilà, the brand changed sex. No less labour-intensive is the "one for the boys" redressing of an existing product. While it might be reductive to suggest that Coke Zero (the bloke Coke that offers all of the taste with none of the calories) is effectively Diet Coke with a butch paint job, the product serves the same basic function. Girls 'diet'; boys 'burn calories'.

The challenge is greatest when the product in question has spent years and millions fixing itself in the mind as a women's brand. But Dove has shown it's possible without resorting to crude gender realignment or high maintenance rebranding. When Dove extended into a men's range the credibility of the move was debated. But the brand extension was targeted narrow, not broad: Brand Manager Paul Connell noted "We recognise that getting the girl and racing fast cars is just not a relevant brand image for men over a certain age. Purchasing personal care products continues to be a chore for many men who can still be found using unisex or female products."[3]

As a brand with a locked-in sense of purity, Dove was well placed to keep things simple. By playing things visually neutral (rather than doing "one for the boys"), Dove Men+Care differentiated itself not just from the mother brand but from the design clichés of the category. Ultimately, the design illustrates the 'change one thing' principle: the white brand becomes a subtle graphite for men (not heavy-handed black or with added 'dynamic' typography). Men are supposed to be simple souls, so it's odd that many brands fail to take such a simple approach to engaging them.

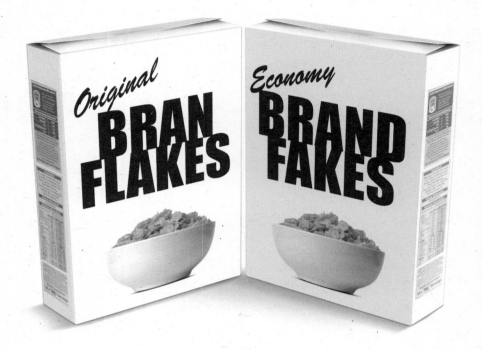

Foxing the supermarket copycats

How many points of difference is the right number? The sharp practice of supermarkets packaging their products to imitate brand leaders shows no sign of abating. The subtext of such designs is always "I might well be made by that big brand to my left – so why not buy my cheaper in-store version instead?" Hence the constant phoney war between brands and their important customers the supermarkets. When a supermarket crosses the line too blatantly, it can expect to find itself in litigation. While for the supermarket imitation is just another competitive tactic, the brands being impersonated need their unique equities to transcend logical price comparisons by shoppers. Sometimes their visual equities are the only thing keeping such brands airborne.

One – ahem – discount supermarket has, so I am told, a specific process to avoid litigation: copy the leader, but design in seven points of difference. This strategy will avoid the serious transgression of trademark infringement. In front of m'learned friend, the colour, typography, shape and so on can each be shown to differ from the source material, even if the end result still looks close enough to trigger the desired associations in consumers' minds.

Brand managers could follow a counter-strategy where their own seven ingredients are all so distinctive in their own right that they frustrate the copycats' attempts to emulate them. But I think this is the wrong answer. If you have seven elements that you believe constitute your equities, it's about four too many. Seven ingredients make a fairly complex soup whose broad recipe can be easily imitated. If, on the other hand, you limit yourself to a simpler design with a small number of distinct elements – such as Coke Classic's flat red, script font and curvy line – it's much harder to produce a copycat. Kellogg's Corn Flakes is really hard to copy since they got the design's mojo back and focused on the rooster. Try ripping off the Guinness can design, which is little more than a colour and an emblem.

So while seven degrees of separation might be right if you're in the business of impersonating brands, three or four is the right target for a brand aiming to be truly distinctive. Being legally protectable isn't the be-all and end-all, but if you can boil your design down to its essentials, not only will you stand apart from the wannabes, you'll also be closer to a (pardon the term) 'iconic' expression of your brand.

Classic

Makeover

Makeover 2

Can brands change outfits without tearing the fabric?

One eternal conundrum for brands is how to refresh while remaining essentially the same. What are the core elements of their image and what are the peripheral details that can be changed?

Subaru has long been a functional engineering-led car. When it elected to have a stylistic makeover, design head Osamu Namba said: "We want to broaden the appeal to make it accessible to more than a small, loyal crowd, we need to add a more contemporary element."[4] It's a design story as old as the car industry. Model T Fords cornered the market, being for their time the perfect functional design for mass construction and mass consumption. But competitors spotted a flaw: consumers get bored and yearn for 'the latest style' rather than a practical but unchanging vehicle. Ford, initially unwilling to bend to such frippery, saw its dominance slip away.

These days, every marque plays the style game, making plain but hardworking Subaru, until the makeover, an anomaly. Online reaction to its new styles was often scornful, with many wishing the company would stick with straightforward substance. Against the received wisdom of the history of car design, was Subaru sacrificing a distinctive niche? Could it have made more capital from being unapologetically anti-designer, rather than introducing lines and frills which make them look like pretty much everyone else? Did refreshing the peripheral elements of its image come at the expense of changing the core of what makes it Subaru?

Sixty-nine years after her debut, Wonder Woman also got a major makeover. The new look was presented as a stronger image with a modern sensibility. But with her bustiere thrust even more to the fore, arguably she looked a bit less wholesome, also less superheroically odd and more prosaically 'real'. In aiming for contemporary relevance, was short-term PR buzz achieved at the price of iconography squandered? It's not her first attempt – in the sixties she was given a mod 'Emma Peel' look.[5] It didn't last and she was soon back in her familiar star-spangled pants. Will history repeat itself?

Household favourite Marmite offers a different approach. It has retained relevance by preserving its famous core pack while constantly innovating and stretching the brand at its edges, with new products, fun promotions and pop-up shops selling Marmite-branded designer gifts. Marmite has used its classic livery as a springboard, rather than seeing it as an anchor holding it back and as such the brand is in rude health. Sometimes brands need the confidence to celebrate what they are, rather than looking over their shoulders at the latest fads and fashions. Marmite has the confidence to work its core image with panache – and that confidence has a charisma which no cosmetic makeover can achieve.

CHARACTERS FOR AN EPIC TALE

Do archetypes ignore life's rich tapestry?

Archetype: the original pattern or model of which all things of the same type are representations or copies.[6] Doesn't sound like a template for a distinctive or epic design does it?

Nevertheless, the use of archetypes as a way of defining a brand's personality is now common practice. Steve Jobs is often held up as a living, breathing brand archetype: the Wizard (of Oz) disappearing behind his curtain then popping back with his latest piece of magic. The burgeoning industry of brand strategy which acts as a comforting tier between marketing and creative briefs makes much play on Jung's theory of archetypes and the distilled mythologies of Joseph Campbell's *Hero with a Thousand Faces*.

But do archetypes really go any deeper than the "If I were a car, what type of car would I be?" approach? Archetypes are reasonably helpful in briefings, but simple personifications are just as effective and don't come with any smoke or mirrors. We were recently briefed to create a logo that was "like Roy Keane" and all the designers got what that meant visually without recourse to an induction in archetypes. Is it possible that archetyping reduces and shorthands the potential depth of personality that can be imbued into a brand, rather than enriching it? Standard diagrams or tools for archetyping offer around twelve basic 'types', such as Outlaw, Jester and Lover. But surely there's a rich cast of more quirky but just as immediate characters. The possibilities are in truth limitless, as the illustration opposite indicates.

Fans of the process might counter "only if you don't understand and use the archetype model properly". But few designers asked to grapple with archetypes will be students of Jung or Campbell, so the output is likely to be a bit shallow. Do such systems really spark imaginative interpretation, or do they risk smothering it?

Leaving aside wizards and warriors, you can always hitch your wagon to someone else's star. Want an archetypically arty/groovy pack? That would be pop art. Want the archetypal pop artist? That would be Warhol. His recognisable style has been applied or referenced by everyone from Marmite to Dom Pérignon, Chupa Chups to Burger King. The results look uniformly 'Warholian', but not distinctively 'of' the brand. Ironic, since Warhol himself was a lover of strong brand icons and the packs he painted were powerful badges long before he turned them into 'art'. Faux archetypal designs offer his stylistic decoration without the strong central branding that Warhol celebrated. Evidence perhaps that 'archetypal' can be synonymous with 'interchangeable' (especially if the archetype is stylistic rather than mythic). The line between archetypes and stereotypes is a fine one.

album

public image ltd.

Even no branding is branding

The 1980s film Repo Man quirkily featured packaging that functionally proclaimed the product – 'beer' and 'cigarettes', with no fancy design. This gag was repeated in the spartan packaging for the PIL album / cassette / CD. What was a visual pun might become a reality: what happens if your distinctive features are surgically removed? The previous UK government proposed to force tobacco companies to sell their cigarettes in uniformly plain packaging (in an attempt to halve the number of smokers by 2020). Some pundits suggested the ban would do little to change hardened smokers' desire to light up, but the strategy was more focused than that: it aimed to reduce the numbers of juvenile recruits.

If you accept that packaging is an effective tool for segmentation and creating appeal amongst the unconverted, then you have to conclude that such a policy would actually be effective. Yet when cigarette advertising was banned, individual brands' market share saw little change. Would this hold true with the removal of branding? If cigarettes were sold under the counter, with no display (as has also been proposed) then the need for branding might disappear entirely. After all, if a seal of consistent quality was the original raison d'être for branding then perhaps in a world where consistent quality is a given, we could return to simpler and more discrete manufacturers' endorsements.

But no branding is still branding: it says in effect "not approved by the authorities or the mainstream". Just the kind of message that would appeal to wannabe teen rebels. Advance demo pressings of records shipped under 'white label' are very cool simply because they carry the cachet of not (yet) being mainstream. The success of Muji (translation: "No Brand Quality Goods") shows that understatement brings cachet and can be the very foundation of good branding.

But politicians like to be seen doing things and pack changes are highly visible demonstrations of activity. Cigarette packaging has already changed massively over the past decade, but can expect still more change yet. Next up, alcohol and snack foods? The best insurance vulnerable brands can take out is to invest in their distinctive iconography while they still can, before their category goes dark. And necessity is always the mother of invention: as communication restrictions tighten, we can expect to see brands trying to preserve their equities in ever more creative ways.

Badly branded birds and global design systems

To become globally famous, brands need to present a coherent face to the world, rather than merely being distinctive within a local context. There is an art to keeping packaging distinctive and idiosyncratic when it has to appeal to many audiences across continents and cultures. A global footprint brings the constant pressure to make the imagery and iconography bland enough to appeal to a very broad market. One solution is to amend the packaging to accommodate local sensibilities, but here perhaps we can consider a lesson offered by nature.

Ever heard of the Trogon family of birds? They are often beautiful and have been knocking around for 49 million years. That should be enough to make an impression, but few of us have ever heard of this particular bird. Their lack of fame is possibly down to their visual inconsistency: 39 species in total, each of which has evolved to thrive in its particular habitat.[7]

The "but my market's different" bleat of the local brand manager aiming to shirk a global strategy will be familiar to many who have endeavoured to create a unified global look for a brand. While not wanting to stray into xenophobia, it is not uncommon to hear UK designers single out French marketers as particularly susceptible to this belief. On a global project for a footcare brand I was told that France's cultural views on verrucas and their treatment were unique within Europe. Vive la différence. At least evolutionary principles rather than maverick office politics is the cause of the Trogon's diversity.

The Trogon is a textbook example of how being inconsistent might be interesting, but is a rubbish way to build a brand. While they've been messing about experimenting with different shapes, sizes and colours, more focused species such as the eagle have grabbed all the attention when it comes to endangered species campaigns, flags, songs and the like. The moral for brand managers: ask if your particular market really does require unique plumage before sacrificing the fame you might enjoy if you stick with the brand's global design strategy.

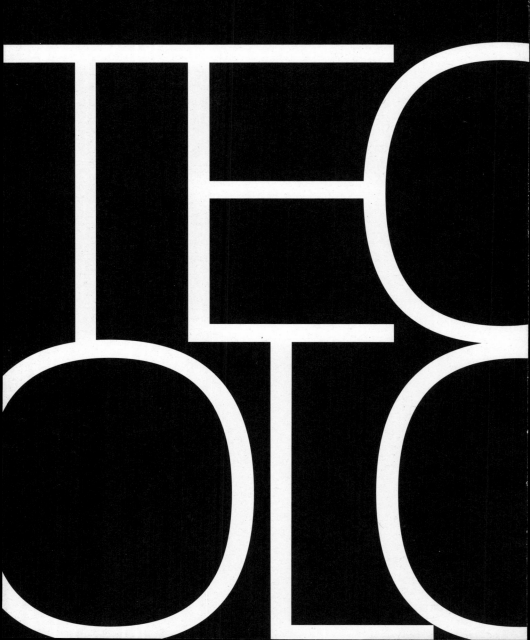

Technology

"*The medium is the message* is a phrase coined by Marshall McLuhan meaning that the form of a medium embeds itself in the message, creating a symbiotic relationship by which the medium influences how the message is perceived." That's a straight lift from Wikipedia, the new medium of knowledge (with a message which, being user generated and updateable in real time cannot be 100% trusted). As technology continues to evolve (at a blistering rate) the media through which we communicate, so the messages themselves will morph and mutate. The challenge will be to keep the messages true to their original vision.

Virtual brands are stepping through the analogue looking-glass

FarmVille's cheesy soft drinks packaging represents one of the most significant evolutions in the relationship between analogue and digital branding in recent years. While leaps in design styling are relatively on the back burner in our era, what we understand as reality (and its attendant rulebook) is being fundamentally shaken. You will probably be familiar with stories about virtual marketing in the avatar-populated Second Life and other alternative worlds. Ad agencies have set up sites therein and you can spend your hard-earned virtual money on virtual products from a plethora of real brands. But with FarmVille's promotion with 7-Eleven, the flow of traffic is reversed. A virtual brand is selling real products in the real world, all with a kickback into the virtual FarmVille universe. It's as if Alice is skipping back and forth through the looking glass.

The 7-Eleven / Zynga (FarmVille's makers) promotion enables consumers to redeem virtual items within the games off the back of real-world purchases. This drives traffic to the games, where Zynga will also charge real money for additional virtual purchases. Meanwhile Small Planet Foods, a subsidiary of General Mills, launched a new brand of organic blueberries in FarmVille. A relatively cost-free innovation is seeded, adopted and so has a justification for investment in the real world. Will more innovation be market tested and previewed in this way?

The breadth of competing brands on a real shop shelf has just expanded to include lots of new-to-market but well established players from another dimension. In design terms these new arrivals come with a visual language all of their own. Will subsequent promotions blend the languages of packaging and gaming to create a whole new category? Watch out for more blurring of real and virtual worlds. Watch out for more interesting branding as a result: brands created by geeks and gamers will be very different from products created by the processes of mainstream marketers in the real world.

Some stats: there is a 30% predicted growth rate in virtual world revenues in 2011. There are 1.1bn visitors to all (175 current) virtual worlds – greater than the population of the US and Europe combined.[8] There is money to be made here and new brands to create. But it's the ultimate in fast-moving consumer goods: the audience thrives on novelty and this year's hot social gaming craze is quickly abandoned for the next big thing. The model to follow is more pop-up shop than permanent bricks and mortar.

Here is a doorway to thousands more words on design than this book had the physical space for.

Will augmented reality mean greater or simpler packaging?

Give consumers too much information and too many choices and they can lose the ability to make a decision. Present information simply and coherently and you help the customer choose. Yet few marketers can resist scratching the itch to 'add value' through product claims, promotional offers and all the other clutter that turns on-pack information into over-information. AR (augmented reality) might mean we will soon be aiming our mobile phones at shop shelves, scoping for barcode-triggered deals, menu suggestions and other goodies. More information, more choices... until we decide this is just more crap to wade through and go back to glancing.

Currently, augmented reality brings us Doritos pack promotions that let you create your very own 3D Doritos Lover monster, upload it onto your social network profile and unleash it to interact with other monsters. AR has brought Robert Downey Jr springing to life on the cover of *Esquire* magazine if you wave it at your computer. We've seen the future – and it's gimmicky. But perhaps as the medium matures, AR will find a more prosaic but useful role. An article about Benetton's *Colors* magazine's AR special[9] suggests one exciting vision of the technology's future. Apparently Benetton's creatives got excited at the possibility of making garments leap from the page. But the guys in accounts spotted the real opportunity: a simple, stylish ad that, via the AR code, unpacks to show rows and rows of product. The classic "more bang for your buck".

Rather than being a vehicle for yet more information and choice, AR could instead be a bucket for all the on-pack dreck that currently crowds out simple information. All the detailed claims, endorsements and legals for promotions could be shunted off-pack. The recipe printed today on the back of pack could instead become an interactive video of a chef's cookery lesson. Promotions accessed through AR could contain all the supporting copy that today chokes up pack faces.

Alternatively, AR can take us to places the brand on shelf might demur from showing us: a giant code was put up in New York that linked the viewer to an online Calvin Klein ad "too hot" to be displayed in public. Packaging tends to be inoffensive, but AR could be a conduit to edgier communication.

Potentially the best designs in our AR future will be the ones that help us make things simpler in the real world and content-rich in the virtual world.

How do you package something which has no form?

Digitally delivered music is seen as lacking value. We are told that most folk under 25 assume the tunes they download should be free. That's about as commoditised as a market gets. In response we see the increasing importance of the 'live' experience to turn a profit. Tours once promoted albums: now the situation is reversed. How is music packaging design responding to the virtualisation of music?

Shown opposite is *The Ecstatic* by Mos Def. As you can see, it would be hard to play it on a turntable. It's sold as a t-shirt with a code to download the album on the hangtag. In a world of declining CD sales, artists have to offer something a bit extra to compete with the intangible world of iTunes and sell (presumably more profitable) physical artefacts. One small band sold a limited edition of $125 dollar 'sculptures' each inscribed with a unique code to download the music. Such designs, aimed at promoting interest for new product in a crowded market, are becoming the music industry's equivalent of the pop-up store.

Technology is polarising music packaging. At the digital end there is no packaging at all. While the in-store physical version does the bare minimum with simple card sleeves replacing plastic 'jewel cases' and elaborate booklets becoming a thing of the past. Such under-packaging also brings a bit of sustainability cred. At the other end of the spectrum is an over-packaged 'coffee table' attempt to add physical value. The Stones re-release of *Exile on Main Street* could be bought for £100 with added books and DVDs. Such inducements presumably target men of a certain age, those who still favour buying their music in physical form but need another reason, because it's probably the third or fourth time they have shelled out for the same basic tracks (from vinyl to tape to CD). Spotify has spoiled £50-man's weekend sweep of HMV and such premium packaged re-releases can act as a replacement fix for his habit.

Online is redefining the way we view products and doing things differently is engaging for consumers. Technology has made it easier for small-scale innovation (born of necessity) to create large-scale effects. The challenge for bigger brands will be to match the imagination demanded of smaller players who have to adapt to survive. But for everyone it's a case of questioning the basic assumptions of what the product's physical form might be: real thinking outside the box.

Feeding the multitudes something palatable

Napoleon "an army marches on its stomach" Bonaparte drove the research and development of preserved foods by offering a prize of 12,000 francs for a successful breakthrough. The winning solution: packing food in bottles, corking them and submerging them in boiling water to stop spoilage. Today's tinned beans are the direct descendant. As we get more people and less land, packaging will soon need to make more such revolutionary breakthroughs.

A set of 21 papers published by the Royal Society[10] spell out a challenging future for food production: a potential need to increase supply by up to 70% in the next 40 years as populations rise. Better preserving technologies and packaging could reduce the 30% to 40% of food waste typical in both developed and developing countries.

But it's the creation rather than preservation of food which opens up new branded vistas. The Royal Society papers suggest a soylent green future of "artificial meat created in a vast vat", which eerily captures the chasm between the possible and the appetising. Meanwhile 'Synthia', the world's first synthetic cell, is surely our most significant new brand. Already tagged as 'designer' by the media and engineered to include a watermark and web address in its genetic code. In time she will revolutionise healthcare and be the fount of new food sources... or lead to the extinction of humanity in scenes reminiscent of the film *I am Legend*, depending which newspaper you read. Brands usually work as beacons of trust and guarantors of predictability. By these criteria, Synthia is an abject failure.

Which brings us to the observation that scientists are not always great at creating brands. The AquAdvantage Salmon is designed to grow at double the normal speed and is set to become the first GM animal we can buy and eat. Assuming its designers have improved on God or evolution (take your pick) and that the fast-growing fish also tastes good, we can look forward to tucking in soon. 'Branded livestock' is nothing new – it's the basis of animal husbandry. Nevertheless this feels like the dawn of a remarkable change in food marketing. But will this new food genre be flagged with a neutrally informative GM flash or with something that spins the science as a positive? In all likelihood the branding of such products will, ironically, be ultra-traditional and conservative, to build trust in Nature 2.0. With this in mind I would recommend that the AquAdvantage is swiftly rebranded as (say) the "Copper-Creek Stone Salmon". Or do we still trust science? The convenient pre-packed TV dinners and quick-cook food products of the 1960s were marketed as futuristic, space-age marvels. Is it possible to replay this card in today's more cynical world?

Are the days of static graphics numbered?

The hype surrounding the iPad's launch might be considered overblown for a "big phone you can't make phone calls on". But it was good enough to impress Rupert Murdoch, who described it as a "game-changer" for the media industry.[11] The iPad, along with ebook readers, is enabling traditional books and newspapers to mutate into animated hybrids of text and video. This is going to change how we view fixed identities forever. One of the big YouTube moments with the iPad's launch came from a demo which took the traditional wood block Tenniel illustrations for *Alice in Wonderland* and brought them to dancing life. This app actually proved slightly more humdrum in the hand, but the software is at the zoetrope stage. We could be at the cusp of a print revolution.

Commercial design's big steps in evolution are typically fuelled by the opportunities afforded by new technology. For example, the bold flat and colourful designs made possible by lithography define the look of the late nineteenth century. Similarly, the loosening of rigid grids as letterpress, with its rectangular blocks of type and image, gave way to the feathered edges achievable with half-tone printing, set the template for looser editorial design as we now see it.

The future of graphics is kinetic. Fixed points are at risk of becoming artefacts. Anything can be retrospectively animated, but the best solutions will have this designed in from the start. As 360 becomes ever more the watchword of integrated branding, it is possible that presenting logos and packs as still points will begin to feel like a primitive exercise and winning routes will be selected on their ability to morph, move and integrate with other filmic elements. The 'limitless variety' approach of AOL's new identity covered elsewhere in this book is an example of branding which is starting to move away from a static representation. The growing presence of animated (so-far silent) 'print' advertising on tube train platforms and escalators is another indicator that movement is becoming the typical expression of branding. All of which ironically puts more pressure on getting the core idea and its locked expression to a powerful and resolved place, so it can take being shaken about while remaining recognisable. Just as Tenniel's iconography for Alice is still unmistakably his one hundred and fifty years on, even when adapted to the latest whiz-bang technology.

Opposite: the first copy of "Alice"
my father bought and the first one
I purchased.

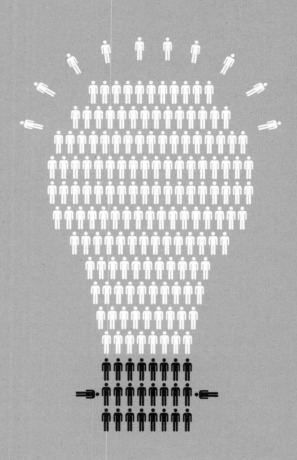

Where are all the good ideas coming from?

Is crowdsourcing just a fancy name for cynically procured free pitching? Or a way for brands to include their customers in the creative process? Perhaps it's just a way of appearing accessible and relevant – and generating a little buzz. Whatever your stance, it's true that ideas offered up for free are often dismissed as valueless (not least by the marketing departments). While customers might give you gold the first time you ask for their contribution, they might not appreciate your coming back for more.

Pepsi showed how smart brands can use crowdsourcing to engage authentically with people. The company cancelled its regular Superbowl ad and diverted the $20 million savings to fund ideas which "move the world forward". These ideas are contributed and voted for online at the Pepsi Refresh Project. 'Cause branding' might seem a cynical ploy to some, but research shows 3/4 of generation Y would switch to a brand they believed to be a force for good.[12]

Real communities that brands can engage with tend to be set up by people, not corporations. Perhaps the best answer is for brands to connect with existing communities rather than spreading their nets wide. Being global but acting local is an engaging strategy, but potentially a headache to orchestrate if you want to tap into local talent. *CreateBrighton* is just one site pursuing this theme. Showcasing lots of great local designers and artists at the click of a mouse, it represents a true creative community. Giving big brands a local sensibility will become far more practical as more sites like this set up shop and using more talent drawn from outside the usual capital city hot spots would be a breath of fresh air.

Meanwhile, big brands' bad ideas are still being launched apparently without regard for their customers' often vocal desire for involvement. Gap's rebrand was universally slammed on launch in the blogosphere and was hastily withdrawn in a kind of reverse crowdsourcing. Embarrassing... unless you believe that Gap never intended to rebrand, but only to provoke a wave of business-building protest from its loyal customers. Now that *would* be cynical.

We quickly mocked up the cans on the right to show how packaging can become more distictive if the usual requirements for navigation, appetite appeal and suchlike are removed.

Will bricks to clicks rewrite the packaging rulebook?

The predicted seismic shift of shoppers from the supermarket to the online environment has in reality taken some time to remake the landscape. Instead many have felt a sense of schadenfreude at famous failures such as Boo. com and other early examples which suggested the new emperor had no clothes. But with Amazon now selling groceries in the UK and M&S declaring a 49% year on year rise in home shopping, it seems the change must surely come.

While it experienced a bumpy flotation, Ocado is a model that promises a game-changing creative and business opportunity. While Tesco et al stock their vans from the same shed that feeds their shelves, Ocado has one über-warehouse (with another planned) from which it processes massive distribution exclusively for online orders. As such it's arguably big enough to warrant and organise bespoke packaging for famous brands: packs which don't need to be designed for shelf standout, or appetite appeal, or invasive hard-sell promotional flashes, because you don't physically see these packs when you buy them (and on screen they can still shout as loudly as they ever did). Packaging was traditionally built for on-shelf browsing. But if the sales game is changing why shouldn't packaging?

Unfettered from the usual clutter and pragmatic requirements, imagine a box of Persil or Pepsi which is designed to grace a kitchen as a thing of beauty rather than as a hard-working brand billboard. If it complements and contributes to your home environment, it will promote loyalty. At the other end of the scale, packs could become truly basic, more sustainable, re-usable and utilitarian. Treated perhaps as refill containers that feed permanent branded storage in the home. Fewer boxes to crush and recycle in this possible scenario. One thing's for sure: a major shift in distribution presents myriad implications and opportunities for the structural and graphical nature of packaging design.

Whilst the experts debate the future scale of online clothes shopping, food (especially predictable, reliable, branded food) is thought by many in the know to be the next likely major player in the online world. As scale of distribution opens up the door for bespoke branding, perhaps now's the time for superbrands to consider how design could transform their packs if the rulebook were thrown in the bin. When you no longer have to stand out, you are liberated to stand *for* something in a much more nuanced but powerful way.

Interactive over-choice:
a design experience we want?

Walter Bender, Executive Director of the MIT media lab noted: "I don't think I've ever seen a piece of commercial software where the next version is simpler rather than more complex."[13] Now Spanish bank BBVA have developed an ATM with a screen experience which is personalised (it remembers you), interactive (lots of touchscreen graphics that are several steps on from the usual basic set of options) and 'entertaining'. The rationale is that in a category which is typically cold and functional, this is a more human and 'delightful' approach, built from the user up.

A Douwe Egberts concept prototype, the BeMoved vending machine, uses motion sensors to turn buying a drink into a physical game for the young at heart. It also allows on-screen click and drag coffee customisation, gives you real-time news and weather and lets you log your personal preferences. All very *Minority Report*. All indicative of the way technology is broadening our choices and pulling on our sleeve to "interact" with brands.

Personally I quite like the cold, simple way of checking my balance and withdrawing cash. I'm not sure I want to be entertained and offered too many alternatives at such a moment. Indeed, the next guy in the queue would probably be delighted if I was as quick as possible. Do technologically driven gimmicks improve or over-complicate our brand experiences? The general drift towards more and more choice and noise is surely creating a space where simplicity will have a certain cachet. Brands with credentials to meet a simple basic need are now offering over-information and over-engineered complexity and seem locked in an arms race. All those accessories and features signify little that will build lasting brand value. What consumers want must always be at the heart of the thinking. We want novelty, but we also want straightforwardness. Or am I out of step with the amount of time and attention folk want to give to buying a vended beverage?

So much for what is bugging me – who do I think is getting it right? The NIKEiD app allows users to take snaps of things they like and convert the colours into a customisable shoe design. As a confluence of trends (customisation, consumer as creative, exploitation of online) the results brew a perfect storm of signifiers for the hot branding approaches of today. But at the app's heart is a single, simple idea: the consumer's real needs for individuality and creative self-expression. As always with new formats, it's the quality of the insight not the complexity of choice that make this initiative memorable.

Words and Symbols

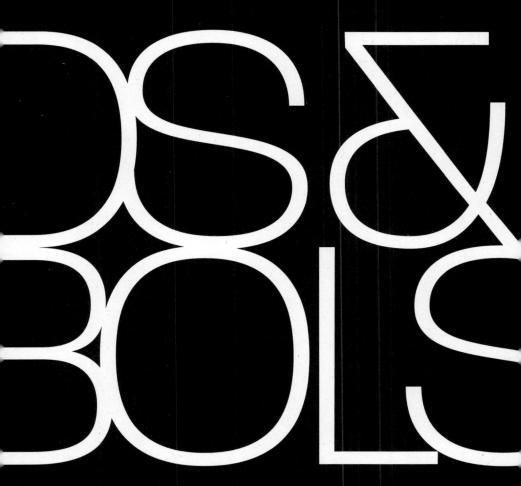

@ dates back to the sixth or seventh century, a ligature meant to fuse the Latin preposition ad – meaning *at*, *to* or *toward* – into a unique pen stroke. Known as *the commercial 'a'* when it appeared on the keyboard of the American Underwood typewriter in 1885, @ then fell into disuse – an overlooked key on typewriters and keypads.[14] If "talent borrows and genius steals" then Ray Tomlinson is a genius. Around 1971 he rediscovered and appropriated @, imbuing it with new meaning and elevating it to a defining symbol of the computer age: it found employment in the world's first email. Now it is part of MoMA's permanent collection, leading many to question how one acquires such a thing for such a purpose?

Symbols and words can change their meanings over time. What follows are some of the ways we currently wield them.

before *after*

below: *the air intake on the controversial Ferrari F1*

What's the meaning of this?

The National Trust recently restored a Tintoretto masterpiece bequeathed to Kingston Lacy house in Dorset. Dull varnish removed and true colours revealed, the Trust appealed to experts to help work out what is actually being portrayed: "There is symbolism in the painting which those in 16th-century Italy would have understood as easily as we recognise the Coca-Cola brand. We've lost that knowledge and are baffled about some of the content." National Trust adviser Christine Sitwell told *The Times*.

There are two distinct and powerful modes of symbolism being referenced here. Firstly, the old masters used symbolism as coded shorthand for the moral of a painting. Secondly, symbolism was used to generate ambiguity. Symbols invite interpretation and therefore, imagination on the part of the viewer. Coke's branding operates in this open-ended way: the logo is a trigger for a broad range of brand associations.

It's interesting to see how fundamentally important and useful these brand cue symbols can be, especially to brands like cigarettes which have limited room for marketing manoeuvre. Marlboro's decision to replace its classic chevron blocks of colour on-pack with linear versions will not have been taken lightly. But why turn one of the world's most recognisable icons into a device which looks like the roof of a house? It's probably more than a stab at contemporaneity of expression. With the threat of legislation that could see all brands share uniformly white boxes (perhaps with little logos at the top if they are lucky), this could be a move designed to make such a transition less abrupt.

Meanwhile, Marlboro experienced hoo-hah on the F1 circuit with many smelling a conspiracy in the Marlboro-sponsored (but legally unbranded) Ferrari. The red, white and black barcode adorning the car reminded many of the sponsor's pack iconography. The press smelt a conspiracy and Ferrari pledged to change the design: "By this we want to put an end to this ridiculous story and concentrate on more important things than on such groundless allegations."[15] Ridiculous or not, cynical or coincidental, the ability to see a chevron in such an abstract design is testament to its symbolic power, achieved through years of consistent application.

The Tintoretto painting will always be more intriguing while it remains enigmatic, just as the best branding suggests, rather than spelling things out. That, of course, also gives brands plenty of wriggle room.

Pack claims and promos take centre stage

Flasher: a man who exposes his genitals in public.

Traditionally relegated discreetly to the corner of a pack, current flash strategy is to let it all hang out. Flake chocolate and Diet Coke both wallpapered their packs with a pattern heralding their respective promotions. While eye-catching and integrated, they arguably achieve this at a cost to their host's sense of stature – more push than pull.

I checked with a few female colleagues (the target for both promotions) and the general reaction to these designs was "bit tacky, bit patronising". Perhaps they simply lack the requisite level of style demanded for such all-over decoration? The US Diet Coke packs promoting heart health were as impactful and on-brand. But they were also effortlessly stylish and had a more universal appeal, achieving a feminine lightness of touch without putting a pink bow on it.

There is much to be said for pursuing simplicity in preference to over-information.

John West tuna puts its strong sales performance partly down to the success of its "no drain less mess" cans. The functional benefits are flagged up via a bold flash with "does what it says on the tin" clarity. It's as traditional a flash as can be found. However its "with no fiddly bit" above-the-line campaign (featuring a forlorn sailor deprived of his chance to play a shanty on his violin) marks this as a flash with big ideas.

Aiding navigation and promoting USPs are key tasks for packaging design. But a fair rule of thumb is that it's more effective to focus on a single message, rather than telling folk everything (which ends up with them registering nothing). Flashes are often the result of two clashing strategic objectives: "give me a pack which expresses our core equities and aids navigation" and "oh, here's a tactical brief – as well as communicating X and Y in our unique tone of voice, please can you also shout about Z as noisily as possible?" How to answer both without the inevitable crash of falling between two stools? John West achieves it in a simple, integrated way. US Diet Coke achieves on-brand standout and differentiation in an untacky and holistic manner. Returning to the pattern designs – the principle was sound. It achieved an integrated solution. But perhaps the execution needed to be better resolved to pull this particular trick off.

WOMEN SPEND ON AVERAGE 94HRS & 55MINS IN THE SUPERMARKET EACH YEAR.

source: Onepoll.com

WOMEN ACCOUNT FOR 85% OF ALL CONSUMER PURCHASES INCLUDING EVERYTHING FROM AUTOS TO HEALTH.

Source: she-conomy.com/report/facts-on-women/

WOMEN FEEL MISUNDERSTOOD !

- **59%** FEEL MISUNDERSTOOD BY FOOD MARKETERS;

- **66%** FEEL MISUNDERSTOOD BY HEALTH CARE MARKETERS;

- **74%** FEEL MISUNDERSTOOD BY AUTOMOTIVE MARKETERS;

- **84%** FEEL MISUNDERSTOOD BY INVESTMENT MARKETERS

Source: she-conomy.com/report/facts-on-women/

"IF YOU MEET THE EXPECTATIONS OF WOMEN, YOU EXCEED THE EXPECTATIONS OF MEN."

Marti Barletta, TrendSight

What (I think) I have learned about Women

With their purchasing power and influence on how family funds are spent, it makes sense to keep on women's good side. Men and women are not so different – men still have nipples after all. But the last thing design wants to do is patronise women. As long as the industry is largely run by men, this remains a danger. Here's what this man has learned:

1. Women are more attuned to colour nuance than men. Maybe it's because while men were off hunting mammoths (big things on the horizon), women were back at the cave picking berries and needing to be more aware of subtle signs of ripeness. In research, women can name: more colours, more elaborate colours and more women can name a favourite colour. Only 0.5% are colourblind to any degree (vs 8% for men). So, avoid overly garish colours – Garnier Fructus' livid green pack was singled out by many women I unscientifically canvassed as a "nasty" design.

2. Women appear to appreciate subtleties of shape, texture and tactility better than men. Nuances such as embossings that would be lost on a man may well be picked up and appreciated by women. Kronenbourg's matt silk Premier Cru bottle made a typical beer suddenly feel cosmopolitan. Girls typically draw rounder scribbles than boys. Not for nothing are curvy Fiat 500s everywhere and in my experience, the driver is typically not a chap. Consider the MAC logo opposite – curved letter ends are the subtle detail which transforms a basic font into something more resolved.

3. Combine the greater appreciation of variety above and it's no surprise women build looks from a wider set of ingredients. Where men are simple souls who want a basic kit of brands, women accessorise and put together looks. How many elements does the average woman combine for an outfit she will wear to a wedding? While men struggle to match a suit and tie. In design terms, Veuve Cliquot does a great job of 'putting together a look' for the brand, with plenty of designer accessories to promote the product, from bar to table to hand.

4. Appreciation of variety also extends to crossing the gender divide. Men struggle to buy 'feminine' design, but women have no such hang-ups in the opposite direction. If you are designing a unisex brand, err on the side of masculine. But if you design in: detail, storytelling, shading and tactility, then your work will be appreciated by women. It will happily be off most men's radars.

As gender trends specialist Marti Barletta notes in the quote opposite, when it comes to design appreciation men are the weaker sex. It's the details which make the difference.

Mascots: brand devices that gain a life of their own

Mascots capture and inject personality into brands. But when they are guns for hire, they can be a tad promiscuous. Paddington and marmalade sandwiches belong together. When Robertson's Golden Shred lured him back from his work endorsing Marmite, Unilever's response to losing their star signing was brilliantly arch: "It seems fitting that a bear as prone to mishaps as Paddington should turn up at Robertson's after developing a savoury tooth," they told *The Grocer*. Flat Eric was developed for Levi's, but the rights remained with his creator Mr Oizo. Subsequently he has rocked up representing *Auto Trader* and in Oizo's music videos. While ITV Digital was a famous miss, their mascot *Monkey* was a popular hit and went on to find further employment with PG tips. Like Premier League footballers, when you hire the talent rather than own it, defection to another team is always an occupational hazard.

Starting from scratch is no guarantee of plain sailing either. The London Olympics Wenlock and Mandeville logos were given a past as the last drops of metal from the stadium's girders. However, this origin story did not save the (certainly far from conservative) designs from a thorough lambasting on their public launch. Style is as important as content and the fact that the blue one appeared to have wet his pants did not count in their favour.

Some mascots develop a life beyond their intended environment. Playboy's logo was originally a stag: the mascot was expediently revised when it turned out the name was taken. Over the years the mark has dramatised and brought to life Playboy's ethos, turned into chairs alighted upon by models, key fobs for the club, emblazoned upon the tail of the brand's jet and of course as inspiration for the bunny girl outfit. Now it appears that the rabbit has transcended the core product. When Playboy Enterprises Inc entered talks with fashion house Iconix Brand Group, the would-be buyer said it was more interested in the company's saucy symbol than the photo spreads of naked women that made the magazine famous in the first place. The magazine, with its declining sales and advertising revenue, they could take or leave. But the brand image and what it powerfully symbolised, was still considered of great value ($300 million was the figure quoted). In an era of online porn, the logo perhaps reflects what we see as a gentler, friskier time which has enormous "naughty but nice" appeal.[16] In the end, Iconix walked away from Playboy – but bought the rights to Peanuts. That's one set of characters which will never grow old.

Can graphics make a car go faster
or put a ball in the net?

While any attention given to design at the 2010 World Cup focused around the debatable aerodynamics of the Jabulani ball, a more subtle competition was occuring on the pitch: both Adidas and Puma have developed bespoke fonts to add numbers and names to their respective team's shirts. Adidas' Unity font was in part derived from the rounded triangles seen on the match ball. It was slim and modern in contrast to Puma's more muscular and dynamic Crepello and Olembe fonts. The Olembe font has a hand-drawn feel that chimed with the looser, less formal spirit of the African teams.

It's impressive that both sponsors showed such attention to detail, but it's a sound investment: fonts are great signifiers of particular eras. These designs will have a long and lucrative afterlife on retro reproduction shirts worn to impress other soccer nerds for years to come. They will be more cherished than any tackily branded vuvuzela. Did the graphics make any difference to the score? Well, the University of Chichester has published research claiming that goalies wearing red shirts are involved in twice as many misses (through saves or blasts off target) than goalies wearing green – proof that looks affect performance.[17]

Every army or tribe needs an identity to rally around. Look at the trouble Hell's Angels chapters take over their jackets. There can be few more emotional arenas to operate in than a football stadium. So even details like shirt markings can potentially add or subtract a little something. Leading teams such as Germany and France seem able to make more experimental graphic choices, while England still goes for a paired down 'spirit of '66" (backwards) look. Have we become the designers of our own limited ambition and subsequent lacklustre results?

In Sven Voelker's book on the graphical decoration of racing cars he explains how the original designs (effectively amateur efforts by the mechanics and race teams) were described as 'war paint'.[18] They were intended to make cars look faster and to intimidate the competition. The finest brand exponent of this art must surely be Martini for Porsche: the cars were unmistakably sponsored by the drink, but the brand livery was brilliantly reconfigured to make the car look streamlined and fast. Paint might not physically make a car go faster, but by underpinning and strengthening team identity and cohesion, perhaps it can help the team give that little bit extra. It's a neat example of how decoration can say 'No.1' before the race is even run and how this approach might give you an edge over the competition. It's only a matter of ink and confidence, whether you're branding a racing car or a pack of biscuits.

Words don't come easy

Copy – which is basically 50% of graphic design – is still a remarkably hit-and-miss part of the branding mix. "Doing an Innocent" has been passé for some time now, but the chatty approach to copywriting is still all around us. When used by boutique brands it can convince, but used by bigger brands and corporations it feels as natural as a rictus smile. New Zealand Airlines' "personality allowed" campaign, where staff debate what specifically makes their airline fab, is a case in point. Why do brands we want to trust for their professionalism – finance, flying, quite important stuff like that – feel the need to express their winsome side? It neither charms nor persuades. The thing Innocent Drinks really did was to be original – a true sign of personality, but a lead much easier to copy in style than follow in spirit. The plastic adoption of their approach across so many brands has the ironic effect of making them all look rather soulless – like a chorus of bad cover versions. Let's also remember that in the real consumer world, Innocent's twee style is regularly sent up for its gag-inducing saccharine style.

Here are two other ways to treat copy: up in the ether is Camper. Barnsley FC's poet in residence Ian McMillan has defined poetry as 'heightened language'. In brand copywriting terms, it's the distinction between harping on in an attempt to evoke an 'authentic' personality and offering something that actually moves the spirit. The shopping bags for Camper shoes say nothing clever. But they look great and if you bother to actually read them they intrigue and transport. Despite deconstructing this kind of stuff daily I have no idea what they are saying, but I don't feel like they are trying to tell/sell me something. Using words as an oblique design element (rather than to inform or otherwise ooze brand personality) feels refreshingly different. Perhaps because so many brands are trying too hard to pull on our coat about what they want to tell us, Camper's approach transcends the language we have come to expect. Or are they just flattering switched-on urban types by having the confidence to prosaically list their colours in an arty-farty way?

Back down to earth, an email from the NHS that gives blood donors the facts they need is factual and straightforward. But it contains one terrific line: "Giving blood is simple and safe and only takes about an hour. Most people hardly feel a thing apart from the satisfaction of saving a life." That's copy with a warm personality which also sidesteps the baby talk.

Standout's vital – but some tricks are best left unplayed

Spanish bank Caixa Catalunya gained plaudits for dramatising a dull 'fixed rates' message with op-art advertising where print patterns appeared to swirl before the viewers' eyes. Given their eye-popping visual impact, it's a wonder packaging has made such little use of op-art trickery. A reasonably persistent Google search revealed slim pickings, beyond the starburst-style graphics found in 1970s detergents and a flattened-out foil from charming Scottish biscuit brand, Tunnock's.

In the sixties there was widespread pirating of Bridget Riley's fashionable black and white paintings. They cropped up on mini dresses, matchboxes and suchlike, but she was far from delighted to see her art appropriated by pop culture. That's about it. In the era of hi-def £70,000 home TVs and 3D movies, is packaging missing a trick, or stuck in a production blind alley?

I believe there are two reasons why op-art hasn't been more exploited. Firstly, while such packs would deliver standout, an op-art focused design would lack the warmth to engage emotionally and the opportunity to add design elements that deliver product relevance for consumers. Not much point in slapping a picture of delicious food in front of a set of buzzing lines. Unless the op-art was used to dramatise the properties of, say, a contact lens solution or painkiller, its use would be somewhat arbitrary.

Secondly, packs are decoded by shoppers at a glance, but op-art requires a few seconds scrutiny before the visual tricks to come alive. We probably wouldn't give them the time they need to work.

Shelf blockings that build into bigger and more impactful patterns are relatively common. Lenticular packaging has been around for a while, but never really taken off beyond tacky packaging for DVD box sets of sci-fi programs. Nobody has really grasped the opportunity afforded by the fact that most packs are approached obliquely, which means perspective can be cheated to the packs' advantage. But perhaps there are limits: packs work perfectly well as they currently operate. Why deviate from a winning formula? Perhaps, like crocodiles, packaging evolved to its optimal form some time ago.

360 integrated branding

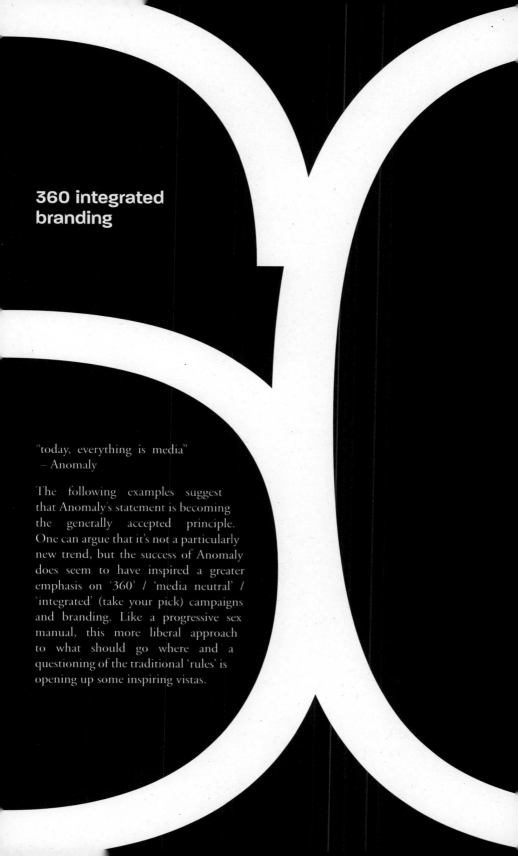

"today, everything is media"
 – Anomaly

The following examples suggest
that Anomaly's statement is becoming
the generally accepted principle.
One can argue that it's not a particularly
new trend, but the success of Anomaly
does seem to have inspired a greater
emphasis on '360' / 'media neutral' /
'integrated' (take your pick) campaigns
and branding. Like a progressive sex
manual, this more liberal approach
to what should go where and a
questioning of the traditional 'rules' is
opening up some inspiring vistas.

*Top: as Barclays intended. Beneath: an example of the ensuing
sticker campaign. The basic branding of the sponsored bikes offered an open
goal to would-be seditionists (or naughty school boys).*

If you are sponsoring a better world, make sure it's appealingly designed

KFC created much buzz around its planned installation of fire hydrants in Indiana. These carried images of the Colonel promoting "fiery" chicken wings. The spin was around good corporate citizenship and smart media placement in a world where traditional advertising messages are losing impact. The media plan must have generated far more free online publicity for KFC than the modest $7,500 investment in branded hydrants itself ever gained. But if the corporate agenda was to create goodwill then there are potential pitfalls – does the world need any more visual clutter? Couldn't KFC be seen to be helping the community without branding said community? If people not only resent the extra visual noise but also question the purity of the sponsor's altruism, such an initiative will backfire.

There was much concern over the dominance of Barclays branding in their sponsorship of London's new hire bikes and cycle lane 'superhighways'. The cycle lanes, in Barclays blue*, represented a huge slug of branding when measured in thousands of kilometres of tarmac. The project, some argued, demeaned the capital, sold the road from beneath Londoners and was a slippery slope to full appropriation of public space for private ends.[19] But the lanes need to be clearly demarcated from regular traffic and Barclays Blue is as good and cheerful a colour to paint the lanes as any other. As for the bikes, £25m means the branding hasn't come cheap and it's this support that's made the scheme possible. But one could argue that Barclays missed a trick by branding the bikes so blandly. Calling the scheme 'Barclays Cycle Hire' and branding the bikes with the basic corporate logo suggests they could have peddled harder in the ideas department. Lack of flair and spirit in such monolithic branding risks making the truly altruistic look merely opportunistic. In a climate where bankers weren't exactly flavour of the month (are they ever?) the big logos were an invitation for an aggressive sticker campaign adding some choice additions to the wordmark. No good deed, it seems, goes unpunished.

If you're set on providing a branded public service, a little flair and imagination might ensure more gratitude. Penhaligon's scented London taxis each smelled of a different fragrance inside and the drivers were trained to talk about the various products. A ride in a scented cab is sure to be an improvement on the usual experience over the summer and it was an impactful use of a tiny budget. But crucially, it brought more to the environment than a garish logo.

---

* an apparent coincidence, as the colour was selected before the sponsorship deal according to some reports.

Making things – it's what brands do

At Glastonbury, the festival's official handheld communications partner (or whatever) Orange unveiled a bit of PR-friendly innovation: wellies which store energy generated by the heat of your feet and use it to charge your mobile. They were probably a godsend by day three without a plug to be found. Glasto is a happy event and this is a perfectly whimsical piece of design that adds a little soul to Orange's sponsorship: they are contributing more to the spirit of the event than an expensively mounted corporate logo. Sometimes silly is as effective as smart.

The closet door handles at the New York office of Havaianas are made from the shoes' straps. Snapped and posted online, a silly (and cheap) idea gets huge positive exposure. A great example of the principle that if you have a design equity, sweat it for all its worth. Someone had a bright idea at Havaianas, got a drill and made it happen. "Living the brand" is personified by such people, rather than those who just nod agreement to the sentiment when it appears on a flip chart. As such, this little detail brings a humanity and charm that most corporate HQs singularly lack.

Product innovation is arguably the ultimate deed in brand creation and therefore the pinnacle of an 'everything is media' approach. But when a brand and its products move away from the context in which they became famous, the core equities need to be clear so the elastic can stretch rather than snap. For example, *Monocle* magazine now has a shop and line of fragrance, but the apple has not fallen far from the tree identity-wise. This jump from authoritative periodical on lifestyle and design to manufacturer of products seems natural rather than opportunistic or random. *Monocle* could do this because it was already a strong brand with recognisable building blocks of visual equity.

What do these projects have in common? It's not just the big idea: it's the consolidation of little ideas around the core that add up to fantastic delivery on a project. Making things rather than spinning claims is a great way to build a brand, be it long-term or stunt by stunt.

The MAC / Liberty co-brand

Do limited edition designs add value or squander equity?

If demand outstrips supply then a brand becomes desirable. But when limited editions become too frequent, they risk diluting rather than bolstering the mother brand's prestige. T.E. Lawrence's publishers proved to be as adept at guerilla marketing as he was at guerilla warfare. *The Seven Pillars of Wisdom*, Lawrence's account of his adventures in Arabia, has a complex history of various published versions. Originally an edition of just 22 copies was printed to secure US copyright in the 1920s. Half went to the author and the Library of Congress. The rest were given an exorbitant price tag of $20,000 to ensure they didn't sell. But these copies were still put to good use, being exhibited in leading bookstores across America. This in turn drove hefty sales for the (only slightly different) $3 version, which must have appeared to be a fantastic bargain in comparison. Limited editions of brands these days share the same agenda of creating publicity (via, in the case of certain sneaker lines for example, similarly impossible-to -attain exclusivity). A design artefact intentionally placed beyond the consumer's grasp is a means of grabbing attention and promoting desire.

Is the Liberty & Co range of premium signature products sold in its flagship store undermined by its mainstream co-branding with Kate Moss / Top Shop, MAC Cosmetics, Nike and Target? Is it a balanced or a schizophrenic strategy? When does brand promotion become over-exposure? At what point does driving volume start having a detrimental effect on a quality brand's sense of value? Liberty's high-end purses and affordable spin-offs inhabit different consumer worlds, although there is an exclusive cachet of location or limited availability in both cases.

Limited editions drive desire by ensuring that demand exceeds supply. But if design equities are stretched too far and too often, they might struggle to snap back to their original shape – and threaten the goose that lays the golden eggs into the bargain. Less, perhaps, means more.

Don't ask what you'll get from a collaboration – consider what you'll give

If 360 is done with soul, it comes over brilliantly. But if it only extends the brand into novel territory in a functional "will this do?" manner, then the initiative tends to smell opportunistic. Applying a brand in an unusual context needs good chemistry and must deliver a 1+1=3 result. That means getting into the spirit of the thing.

Dulux's Let's Colour initiative hits this spot. The company makes paint, and colour can transform. So far, so obvious. But they add this to a gap not many brands fill. Much 'corporate social responsibility' fails to leverage the middle word – social. Typically the desire to do good comes over as rather more corporate than personal. Dulux, in a bid to "banish the grey", has begun a global initiative to brighten up dreary spaces with both employees and community getting their hands dirty. The end results are uplifting, engaging, accessible, creative, transformational and a great advertisement for the product. We're inspired to see how our homes could be equally transformed via grander examples from around the world and the initiative connects an idea with real people and places in a global way.

Dulux has won plaudits and plenty of attention for its activity. The most important place a 360 campaign has to operate is within people's imaginations. As branding it exists on TV, a dedicated website, Flickr and so on. But to make it live and to gain entry into hearts and minds takes spirit, not just a good logo.

Small runs can make big impressions

The scale of effort and time involved in using the unwieldy beast of packaging for tactical ends means it can feel like a big idea is required to justify the trouble and expense of specially produced packaging. But there are examples which show packaging can be produced in a more limber manner.

Coca-Cola Hong Kong has smartly exploited the fact that in Asia red is traditionally a colour of happiness and good fortune to create specially designed wedding cans. Only available for sale to Chinese wedding banquets, the cans have fast become collectors' items. It's an interesting example of a superbrand thinking and acting small and local, but in a manner entirely in line with the brand's global personality.

Similarly Pepsi created designs for a single day event: Halloween. Typically when a brief comes in for, say, a Christmas edition it is described as 'seasonal' because stock will still be on sale through January. This tends to dilute the potential impact (a general wintry theme rather than one aimed squarely at December 25th). But with digital printing enabling shorter production runs, perhaps micro editions have a big future for any brand with the energy to sustain them?

Small ideas can leave a big impression if they really integrate themselves with an event or opportunity. In Japan, "Kitto Katsu", meaning "surely win", is a phrase students use to wish each other good fortune in their exams.[20] Nestlé's pounced on this by teaming up with Japan's Post Office to produce Kit Kat chocolate postcards, encouraging a more personalised and indulgent delivery of the Kitto Katsu message amongst this enthusiastic audience. The promotion was so successful, selling 250,000 units, that the product has now become a permanent feature in Post Offices. It's an inspiring example of a brand not just opportunistically catching onto something, but taking it to another level by creating a tangible product that builds on the idea. Particularly in the Asian culture, where there is concern that festivals and local expressions of identity are under threat from globalisation, it's an approach designed to win friends and influence people.

Although relentlessly releasing limited editions can risk diluting the core brand, such micro editions which celebrate a particular event or topic can facilitate a surprisingly personal dialogue between brand and consumer.

If the face fits, use it

Ever since Max Factor secured the publicity services of screen goddesses from the silver screen (and became rich on the results) famous faces have imbued brands with reflected glamour. Dita Von Teese becoming "the face of Perrier", at first glance, looks like nothing more than another business opportunity for the burlesque artist and 'muse'. She's worked with Wonderbra, collaborated with Moschino and Viva Glam and a bunch of others.

But in a world where brands attempt to pose as archetypes, Von Teese is the real deal. Archetype is what her act is all about. By using her, Perrier shorthands itself as a bit sophisticated, European (even if she's American) and edgy. She's also an 'artiste', so the partnership comes across as a creative collaboration. Simply layering her visual style onto the can does the rest. In other words, she isn't just bringing her fame to collaborations, she's bringing her style – and the designs appear distinctive as a result. Meanwhile, a film of her sashaying around the interactive Perrier Mansion is a neat extension of her image that adds depth and content to proceedings.

While George Clooney holding a cup for Nespresso looks generically glamorous, Von Teese doing something similar for Perrier is the smarter buy because she comes with a distinctive style built-in. The best tie-ins are those where the star has established iconography (rather than just having a famous face) that can be blended with the brand equities to create a convincing association.

Similarly the latest in a long line of Diet Coke fashion editions came from the pen of Karl Lagerfeld. With such ventures you sometimes have to wonder who is doing whom the favour. With shameless chutzpah, Lagerfeld leaves us in no doubt on this occasion. Since he famously went from being somewhat portly to his current svelte profile, the designer has often represented himself as a bit of a logo. In this case it makes sense, unapologetically announcing the tie-in and has a subtle relevance – he supposedly drank quite a bit of the stuff while losing the extra pounds. The best brand marriages are ones where the partners are selected judiciously for such simpatico values, rather than just their general level of fame.

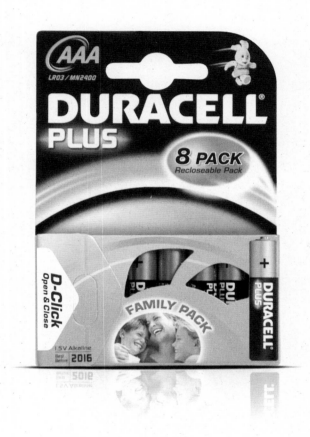

Did the D-Click Duracell design hide its light under a bushel?

Never mind the picture, look at the frame

Good storytelling is the vital frame which contextualises any design's merits. And without a good frame, there is always the danger the picture will be undervalued.

Two recent and rather neat pack physicals: a Heinz Tomato Ketchup sachet you can squeeze or dip and a resealable Duracell battery box which prevents the batteries rolling around your man-drawer. Such design work is not usually thought to belong at the cutting and glamorous edge of design. It can be easily overlooked, despite the fact it offers huge added experiential benefit to the consumer. Typically, technical innovations of this kind lack the buzz of a sexy (if cosmetic) graphical makeover.

Such is the case with the Duracell D-Click pack, launched with no big PR piece, a very low-key presence on the brand's website and on-pack communication which looks, politely, to have been produced in-house. Conversely, Heinz's sachet seems to be setting itself up as the answer to the prayers of anyone who has suffered a dip/squeeze conundrum. Online, you can even watch a film of the sachets on the production line – heady stuff. While the Heinz PR might be a little OTT, it got results: national press coverage and tonnes of links online (in contrast to the online void that is Duracell's D-Click). Heinz succeeded because it integrated the innovation into a very resolved piece of branding and recognised that the little things can mean a lot. Meanwhile Duracell, which has solved a genuine consumer problem, appears to have missed an opportunity with equal potential.

Framing is so powerful an effect that you always need to be careful how you set up a proposition. If a design reminds a client of, say, "a wonky rocket", then the name will inevitably stick. Here words are giving the design an unflattering frame. Referenced in a couple of meetings, this label will kill a design stone dead by giving something perfectly sensible a bad name. When you're the victim of inadvertent framing and the victimised design is one that's close to the agency's heart, it's essential to rephrase and reframe as fast as possible. Nothing like thinking on one's feet...

"They don't make 'em like this anymore."
The UK Hoover manufacturing plant, built in 1932. Now a Tesco, it was beautiful enough to inspire an Elvis Costello song honouring its splendour.

Should brands shout their names from the rooftops (or be discreet about their addresses)?

It's odd in a time when 'every consumer touchpoint' forms a link in joined-up design strategy that the brand's home is often the most neglected aspect of its presentation. The factories producing our best-loved brands are rarely oil paintings. A fortune can be spent advertising a beer's artisinal charms, only for the image to be undermined by the brand's logo proudly mounted on giant, gleaming tanks set in an industrial wasteland.

Such branding doubtless shows a sense of pride in production and no brand's true origins should become a guilty secret. But there's something to be said for letting consumers pass by in blissful ignorance. Consider the Lyle's Golden Syrup plant in east London. A towering monolith with giant chimneys belching smoke, it does little to enhance the impression of a brand seemingly unspoilt by progress. So, why the enormous branded signage hung down its flanks? When the brutal truth fails to live up to a brand's carefully polished image, it might be wiser to signpost the buildings more discreetly.

Yet while factories are not obvious candidates to play the sexy shop window, it is possible. Take Guinness' Storehouse for example. Effectively a museum for the brand at the brewery's site, it's a justly popular destination for Dublin tourists and acts as a great advertisement for the stout. It could have been just so much Victorian bricks and mortar, but it has soul and theatre. The lines of eager visitors must include many future evangelists, so it's arguably a shrewder investment than any particular piece of TV advertising. Similarly, a visit to the Budweiser brewery in St Louis is a powerful induction into that brand's scale and idiosyncrasy. From the dalmations employed to keep the Clydesdale horses calm to the quirkily decorated and spotless brick buildings where the beer is brewed. You can't visit this site and dismiss the beer as "too big to be interesting".

Innocent's 'Fruit Towers' creates personality and myth around the factory through back label copy, factory sight-unseen. Both they and Google have made some play of showing off their climbing walls and ping pong tables, the better to demonstrate the grooviness of their working days. This corporate mythology reaches its pinnacle in the towering white castle and general design of Disneyworld – the original destination 'brand embassy'. Substance at the factory can also build strong mythology: think of the legendary banked test track on the roof of Fiat's Turin factory.

These are all examples of brands which project their souls through their bricks and mortar. They show that if you have solid foundations, it's possible to build great and lasting brand communication.

Doing the right thing?

Honest, decent and true – watchwords
for building trust in brands. Life used
to be so much simpler for marketers
who just got on with the business
of selling. Now, consumer pressures
combine with legislative mandates to
create a world where brands need to be
good citizens, not just good salesmen.

How do you brand bad news?

The answer, typically, seems to be "you don't". When the proverbial hits the fan for a brand, it's common to hear criticism in the media that the corporate response is slow to arrive and fails to give appropriate clarity and reassurance. The best approach is to keep PR materials as direct but as bland as possible. This not only reflects the gravity of the situation and signifies the company's willingness to stand up and be counted, but makes the topic as visually unmemorable as possible. The corporation takes the hit to protect, as much as possible, the brand image. A fast response which leads rather than follows in the online sphere and connects globally, is also smart. This helps consumers give you the benefit of the doubt and puts you on the front foot.

Toyota UK was criticised for failing to quickly run any marketing activity specifically addressing its product recall following the various pedal-related incidents. The company's homepage was still in selling mode days into the media hoo-hah, with the recall information tucked almost invisibly away at bottom left. Toyota also continued to run a 'swap scheme' advertisement with the priceless line "Can't scrap it? You could swap it" emblazoned above pictures of their cars. In the US, Toyota was a bit quicker off the mark, with plain-speaking and proactive messages quickly added to the website. Importantly, the approach in the US was along 'content is king' lines, with no badging or adornment of the messages that risked cementing the issue's association with the brand in the longer term.

Then there are situations where the branding itself becomes toxic. As BP continued to fail in controlling its leak, a slick of parodies of the logo seeped into the collective consciousness. Elegant and green-leaning, the brand's *Helios* symbol was intended in part to signify the company's ambitions "beyond petroleum". No need to labour the irony. But some of the (much reproduced in the media) parodies strayed far from the topic and were reprinted with little context or explanation of their meaning. For example, the image opposite referenced a famous photograph of an execution during the Vietnam war. BP clearly don't execute people. What had this to do with an oil spill? Nevertheless, this adaptation of BP's logo showed up all over the press, with no editorial context added beyond "here is evidence of people's anger towards BP".

It's going to be interesting to see if BP will attempt to rehabilitate its image via its current identity, or will instead be forced into an ignominious rebrand. Any brandmark is a hostage to fortune and this fantastic identity became a powerful shorthand for failure and all manner of ills.

As sustainability measurements standardise, the truth will out

The World Economic Forum's 2010 meeting at Davos featured discussion over a proposal to standardise designs that denote the carbon and water footprints of products and their packaging. While yet to become a reality, a universal system (presumably some graphical device with numbers) would offer consumers the benefit of simple, comprehensible information and offer brands the chance to clean up their packs. Currently, myriad brand-led sustainability messaging continues to pop up like measles, potentially confusing consumers and cluttering designs.

One downside of a universal system however is that it might quickly become a much easily overlooked graphic wallpaper. Whereas brand-led initiatives can offer information in engaging and distinctive ways. Universal or bespoke, the big challenge is to make footprint information graphically understandable. For example, is an 80g carbon footprint on a pack of crisps a reasonable or awful thing? Those of us without a mathematical or scientific brain need visual analogies or comparisons to make the numerical meaningful. Or failing that, a crude good-to-bad universal rating measured against industry standards.

The proposed Eco Index might play a role here. Which jeans are 'greener', Levi's or Wrangler? These brands, alongside Nike, Adidas, Target and others are aiming to agree common criteria to rate the greenness of their products. A bold move, as it might, for example, give an Adidas sneaker a gold rating and an equivalent Nike sneaker a bronze. As the Prius proves, this is enough to strongly influence some consumers' choice. While still in development – it's necessarily complex, looking at the whole lifecycle of products from materials, to transport, to disposal – the index is already acting as a catalyst for change. Some participants are already changing their systems in light of the scheme, in order to improve their scores. Such universality is significant, as currently brands can simply talk up their good points, allowing for plenty of disingenuous wiggle room.

Standardised green measurements are surely coming. So what are the implications? Above all, brands will have to walk the talk. But unlike the straightforward business of, say, counting calories, any green scoring will be more subjective and aggregate factors which may not reflect the way consumers think. Is an expensive gold standard green trainer produced in the UK better than a responsibly produced 'developing world' trainer sold at half the price? And if the UK version, slightly behind on points, promises a proportion of the price will be reinvested in green projects in the developing world, then which one nets out as the greenest choice? Change is coming, but the answers are not going to be easy.

blue
sky

HARD
FACTS

Getting going is half the battle

Once upon a time, sustainability ideas were punted to clients as the meeting closed. Typically any appetite for change was "for next year". Clearly that's changed, but the next phase was as ineffectual: enthusiastic workshops with 'blue sky' ideas that were then headed off at the pass by the production experts. The easily discouraged stalled.

It was a teething phase. Those ideas were not truly blue sky, just well meaning but ignorant and they fell between two stools: the practical and the truly revolutionary. My observation is that there are two fruitful places to start any CSR thinking. The first is: "What can we do today?" To answer this, involve those production experts. Get them to present what's possible. And which ideas will save, not cost money. Then it's the role of design and marketing to take these (sometimes seemingly dreary) start points and turn them into compelling, creative, brand-centric activity. Sustainability innovation often feels like it's required rather than wanted – not the most positive foot to step out on. If the solutions aim to use the sustainability issue as a catalyst for generally stronger branding, then the outlook becomes less overcast.

The second place is true blue sky – for example: "What if our packaging was banned altogether?" This silly line of enquiry will take you to some inspiring places for brand distribution, behaviour and so on.

Now it's time to sell the ideas up. The magic words are "pilot scheme" and "prototype". In other words, don't try and boil the ocean, but aim to get some commitment to tangible progress. "Cheaper" is also persuasive.

The best advice I heard came from Eugenie Harvey, one of the team instrumental in launching the Anya Hindmarch "I'm not a plastic bag" bag. It launched with a fantastic amount of publicity and Harvey went off on her honeymoon. On her return the negative backlash had begun. Her view: "perfect is the enemy of good". In other words, you are not going to nail it all, but getting started is indeed the best start.

Once under sail the most effective companies are those which generate more initial ideas and then develop them for longer. In other words, they have a bigger funnel and it stays wider for longer. Once you start, don't stop.[21]

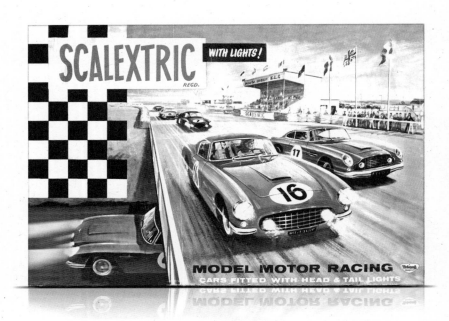

Toy packaging featuring exciting artists' impressions: an evergreen approach.

When you can't believe your eyes, it's time to worry

One of the biggest (yet subtlest) changes in our world has been the rise of Photoshop. From fuss over Cameron's 'airbrushed' election campaign portrait to photojournalists being sacked for manipulating their shots, we live in unbelievable times. Retouching and airbrushing are nothing new, but Photoshop's ease and accessibility have helped restraint and common sense go out of the window. Over-zealous retouching has become the lampooned target of popular sites such as PhotoshopDisasters. Brands are at risk: if consumers can't trust the promise, they can't trust the brand. The real skill required by today's technicians and marketers is the art of restraint. That means having a good eye for proportion, detail, lighting, colour – all the things, ironically, that a decent realist painter might have.

Debenham's has moved away from retouched models to more honest shots. Cynics might see a manufactured 'issue' in this initiative (the poster girl for the initial experiment was still naturally as close to perfection as one gets), but it chimes with politicians' naive calls for any retouched shots to be accordingly labeled. Naive because this in all likelihood would mean every shot currently in the commercial sphere. We all know that every model and famous face in every magazine doesn't share the same plastic sheen because of a quirk of genetics and there can't be a food photograph on a pack in the UK which has not at least been digitally colour-corrected. Photoshop gives customers what they want: 'reality' served up sans zits or blemishes.

Away from high end retouching but still a territory of image manipulation, contemporary toy boxes haven't changed significantly since the 1970s 'artists' impressions' which promised more than the toy was ever going to deliver – all decodable to an informed adult eye, but as persuasive to an easily excited nipper as ever. Today, as then, the box is always half the fun and perhaps being let down by a product which does not deliver on the packaging promise is a sad little lesson best learned early. But it's surprising that while we hear much about advertising standards in such communication, the reality seems so little changed on pack. Here, it's less about invisibly manipulating an image, more about blatantly dramatising the product in the mind's eye.

Legislation and a general desire for products to look natural rather than synthetic have actually seen a big reduction in the extent of retouching demanded by clients – less is definitely more. The days of 'plastic' food visuals and suchlike are numbered, but my advice to brand managers is to keep a sharp eye on visuals, lest you lose consumer trust or end up a Photoshop disaster.

Is sustainable luxury an oxymoron?

Sustainability and luxury are not obvious bedfellows. Indeed "excessiveness… darling" has become synonymous with luxury. Chanel built a 265 tonne iceberg for a recent Paris show: "made from ice and snow imported from Sweden, it was 'recycled' afterward by being returned there in yet another gas-guzzling journey," according to *The New York Times*.[22] Elsewhere Karl Lagerfeld said that[23] "the environmental activists had a point but should learn to dress better". Generally speaking, extravagant art directors thumbing their noses at issues that concern us all seems an unsustainable policy. While some luxury brands are realising their consumers might not want to associate with brands which make them look like planet-eating airheads, the majority of category-leading brands are missing a golden opportunity to design with substance as well as style.

The perceived shallowness of luxury brands is seen in even starker light in emerging markets. The attitude that we're dealing bling to tasteless oligarchs says more about us than it does about them. Different cultures have nuanced attitudes to luxury that can reveal our own conceptions as parochial and arbitrary. The Chinese, for example, associate luxury goods with a deeper culture of 'face', or personal reputation. Meanwhile billboards for luxury goods were removed by the mayor of Beijing, who said they were "not conducive to harmony". Perhaps we should reconsider the strategy of slapping on Swarovski crystals and gold to seduce the eastern consumer?[24]

There's no inherent reason why exclusivity can't also be green.

Luxury brands operate at a profit margin that can afford responsibility. Luxury is partly about application of intensive and well-rewarded human craft rather than mass production. What if craft and workmanship drove value rather than expensive materials and over-packaging? After all, minimalism has cachet. An exclusive line consumes relatively small amounts of raw material, so communities of craft workers could produce beautiful, desirable and profitable objects that cost little to ship around the world. But luxury brands are still applauding themselves for moving to FSC paper, or worse, continuing to fiddle while Rome burns. Leaders in fashion and quality could be leaders in sustainability too.

Order #F-0174
05/12/10 12:49pm
1135 NE MLK Blvd. Portland, OR 97232
(503) 235-6858 www.burgerville.com

Fresh ▸ Local ▸ Sustainable

NUTRICATE (nu-tri-kAt) v. To nutritionally educate.
receipt

Qty	Item	Price	Calories	Fiber(g)	Fat(g)	Carbs(g)
1	HALIBUT SANDWICH BASKET	$7.09	-	-	-	-
	Halibut Sandwich		490	2	27	43
	No Tartar Sauce		-132	0	-14	-1
	Side Salad		50	2	3	4
	Bleu Cheese Dressing		150	0	16	1
	NUTRITION TOTALS		558	4	32	47
	% DAILY VALUE - 2000 CALORIES		28%	16%	49%	16%
	% DAILY VALUE - 2500 CALORIES		22%	13%	39%	13%

```
        Sub Total         $7.09
            TOTAL         $7.09
             CASH        $10.25
           CHANGE         $3.16
             PAID         $7.09
```

Did You Know ❷

Burgerville offers a variety of
great-tasting dressings to choose from. Try
our Raspberry Vinaigrette, Honey Dijon, or
Lite Ranch -all under 100 calories!

Trust – a free but priceless commodity

In our age of internet scrutiny, honesty and rigour are essential. The back label of a chocolate syrup pack boldly proclaims the benefits of calcium. While, millimetres lower, notes in the small print that it provides "0%" of your daily calcium needs. This perceived evidence of duplicity subsequently travelled far and fast online.[25] It might have simply been an unfortunate typo. But the audience is unforgiving – an innocent mistake or not, this is a good example of the need to dot i's and cross t's. Trust is always one small mistake from being squandered.

Regulators such as the FSA (Food Standards Agency) provide a safety net for design agencies servicing the food industry. When journalists naively ask designers "what tricks do you play to get around legislation and hide the real nature of a product's nutritional facts?" they suppose we are skilful dissemblers playing a game of duplicity. Actually, as any fule kno, that's a highway to brand disaster and truth well told is by far the smarter option. However, designers are not trained nutritionists: we assume that the facts we are given to communicate are essentially true and thanks to the FSA, designers can point to a body whose existence allows us to presume this to be the case.

The smartest brands are those which appreciate the value of honesty and transparency, with no need for watchdogs official or self-appointed. Burgerville (a fast-food chain which endeavours to feature seasonal, local ingredients) provides till receipts complete with a full nutritional breakdown of what you just ordered. How many of their global competitors would be so keen to pass over a tray of their produce with such a synopsis of what it adds up to in calories, salt and fat? Even if customers choose to ignore Burgerville's information, the very act of presenting a full disclosure is reassuring: it shows the chain cares.

If you're buying a burger, you've already made your health and nutritional choices, right? Burgerville shows self-confidence in its approach and credits the customer with intelligence. Treat brands that are unashamed of their nature will build more trust than those who stick their heads in the sand. But it is products like cereals, which sit somewhere in the no-man's land between health and treat who have most to clarify. They often seem to be talking up their fibre while demurring to proclaim their sugar content and suchlike – in the interest of preserving trust they need to be more honest with themselves and with consumers. All must wield design to clearly express where they truly stand.

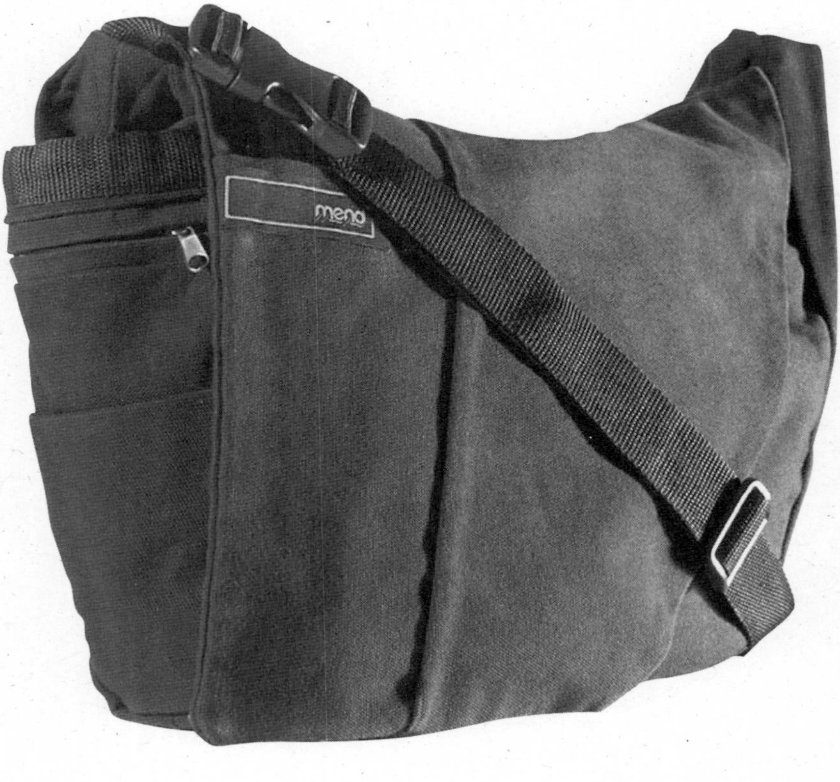

Image courtesy of Invisible Children, Inc.

Logo, actually

Much has been made of the anti-corporate "No-Logo" generation, who reject the McCulture of a corporately, spoon-fed lifestyle. But these consumers are really quite different from their seventies predecessors. The 1970s counterparts were genuinely No-Logo: itchy home-knitted jumpers and wonky self-thrown crockery. The Good Life was not a designer choice. One definition of the difference between the post-war make-do-and-mend generation and ours was that they spent time to save money, whereas we spend money to save time.[26] Today's spoilt (if goodhearted) ethical consumer might be looking for alternatives to the big brands, but when pursuing ethical lifestyles and consuming ethical brands they still want brands per se.

Happily, the world of online shopping is bringing our cosy world and brands from more challenging environments into closer orbit. Ethiopian shoe company soleRebels sells funky shoes made from recycled truck tyres and locally produced textiles. Distribution via Amazon and suchlike means they can be based in Addis Ababa but "act American" and profits are being invested in a solar-powered factory. SoleRebels' founder told *The Guardian* that while the new factory "will better showcase the company's eco-friendly methods, that's not the main reason customers like the shoes. People buy soleRebels because they are good, not because they are green or from Ethiopia. Our product speaks for itself."[27]

Mend sells bags produced by a workers' collective. They look cool and are a responsible choice. Each label carries the name of the woman who actually made the item. Working for Mend is presented as a great second chance for people who live in a part of the world where things are much tougher than most of us can imagine. Local narratives and traceability as part of the brand promise make for a more interesting brand: it's a responsible product on one hand, a visually cool brand on the other.

All wonderful and positive, but also evidence that the No-Logo generation of consumers is just as badge-conscious as their mainstream counterparts. It's just that the badges being flashed are thought to be alternative – arguably a subtle form of 'one-upmanship' and display of piety. Today, No-Logo really means Right-Logo. Nothing wrong with that: it means our jumpers aren't scratchy, our crockery looks attractive and we have the choice to pay decent people a decent wage.

Little ideas, big claims and real change

Against a trend for little ideas dressed up as sustainability breakthroughs comes the pictured sharpener for a razor, which can extend your reusable blade's life by many times. The flaw, if you are in marketing, is that it would lead to falling sales in disposable razors. This is presumably why it's not being promoted or adopted by a male grooming brand. It brings to mind the Alec Guinness movie *The Man in the White Suit*, where the hero invented a dirt-resisting and incredibly strong fabric – a boon for the common man struggling to make ends meet. The combined interests of the unions and the factory owners ran Guinness out of town. Surely the time is ripe for a brand to grasp the opportunity to re-invent category rules by brave innovation. If you championed the longevity of your blade, you could own the thought-leading high ground and charge a premium.

Puma's "clever little bag" uses 65% less cardboard and has gained a tonne of press – probably because it looks so damn cool. Puma has turned packaging reduction to its design advantage: every detail has been considered and aesthetically resolved. Similarly, UPS launched a reusable, resealable envelope – an attractively designed execution of a simple idea. Each envelope is made from 100% recycled fibre with 80% post-consumer content. Coupled with its fuel-efficient fleet – UPS drivers logged 77.3 million miles more than they did ten years earlier, but used 3.2 million gallons less fuel[28] – customers can believe UPS is trying to affect changes big and small.

The rigour of these solutions impresses and elevates them above the ranks of little ideas strutting around with puffed-out chests. If you can't think really big, at least think in beautifully styled and integrated detail.

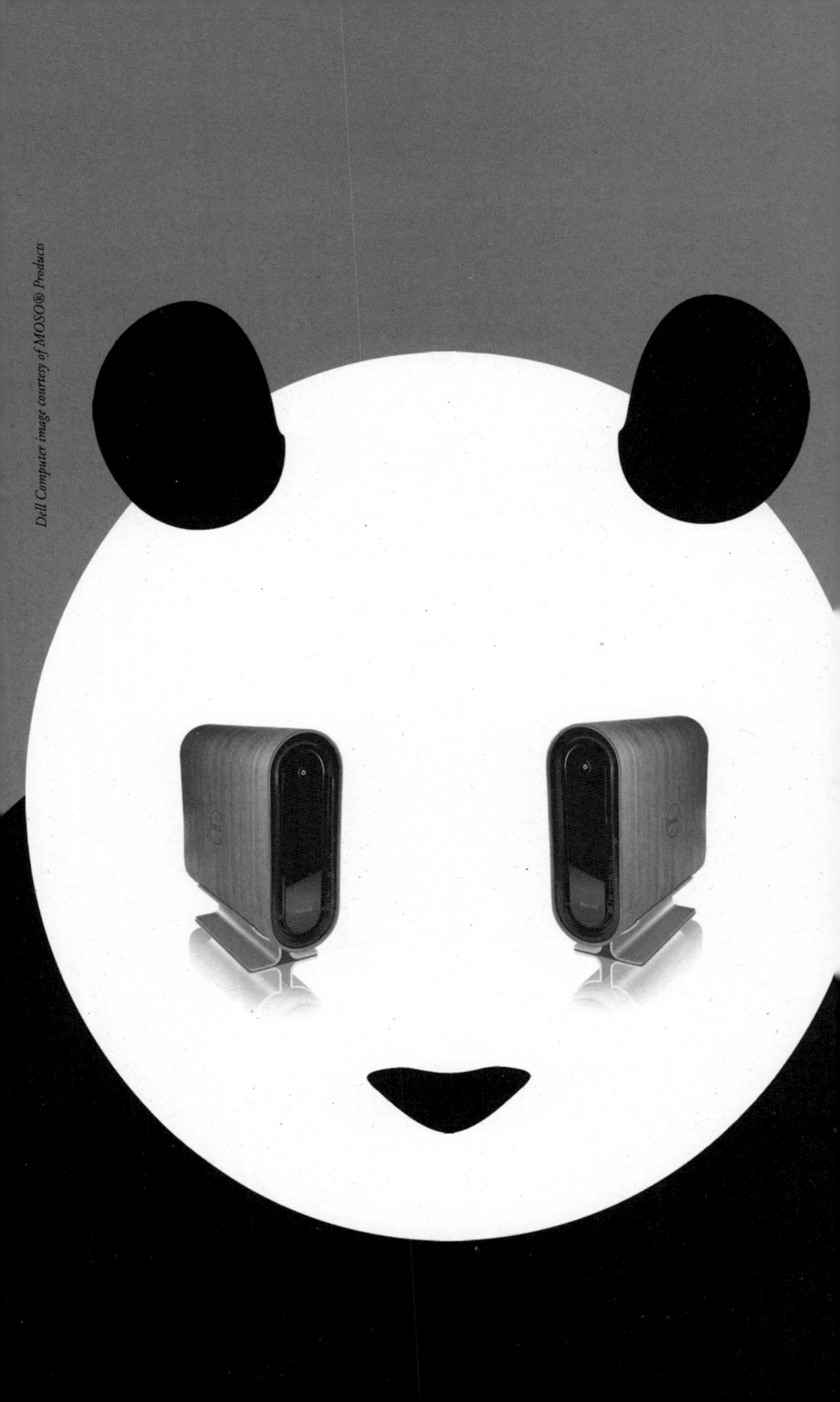

Dell Computer image courtesy of MOSO® Products

The best sustainable thinking is bold and joined up

The best sustainability design initiatives combine sound design thinking and careful branding to elevate good ideas to the holy grail of 'thought leadership'. To pull this off requires thinking differently, but also thinking things through.

For example, Dell has been producing computers with a bamboo cladding for a little while. The woody effect offers a distinctively warmer and more crafted feeling alternative to the category's usual glossy plastics.[29] The next step is to replace some of its packaging (such as the moulded cushions used to protect the laptop in transit) with bamboo as well. The upside? As a fast-growing grass, bamboo offers a sustainable material kinder to the earth's resources. It's also a cheaper manufacturing process which is mechanical rather than chemical. Dell has covered the downsides: the raw material is certified by the Forest Stewardship Council and is not grown with the aid of hazardous pesticides. The factory is in China, close to the bamboo (but the bamboo is farmed far from the grazing grounds of the giant pandas). Most municipal authorities currently don't recycle bamboo, but the company is in the process of helping change this. The only snag might be scaling up operations if it takes off. The innovative approach with a close eye on detail yields not just more sustainable packaging but also a more distinctive brand behaviour. This in turn relates to a signature Dell product, building an impressive piece of joined-up thinking.

Another line to connect is that between consumer insight and the innovation pipeline. The Audi e-tron is a prototype all-electric car. While such concepts rarely see the light of day, there seems to be serious intent to make this one happen. What's interesting in the concept is the understanding that Audi's consumers are not prepared to compromise on what they love about the brand. The press release focuses, as does the design, on performance first, electric power second: "Imagine a new Audi supercar. 0-62 mph in just 4.8 sec. 230kW and 4,500 Nm of torque. Incredible looks. Its four motors drive each wheel individually, making it a true quattro. This new Audi is a classic – instantly taking its place in the ranks of the world's most exciting automobiles and it runs on... electricity."[30] The stumbling block, obviously, will be in creating a production version of the battery which gives the car a decent range. But, we're assured, they're working on it. The benefit for petrol-heads is very fast acceleration. So, potentially a future where green issues can be sold to the decidedly un-green 'Clarkson' demographic. This approach is brand first, electric second – a smart move away from the suspicion that electric cars are probably rubbish!

Such ideas, especially resolved, brand-centric, relevant ones, are contagious.

Can bad taste make good branding?

It's a trendspotting truism that big trends create scope and opportunity for counter-trends. So it's no surprise that 'irresponsible' branding has emerged in a world of increasing brand responsibility. Doing the wrong thing can stand out when your competitors are sanctimoniously toeing the line. Here are a couple of brands that ostensibly play up to a bad boy image. But as we know from our schooldays, bad boys get plenty of snogs behind the bike sheds...

BrewDog court controversy with their beer End of History. 55%, £500 a bottle and stuck in your very own stuffed animal. It looks designed to appeal to Damien Hirst rather than responsible drinking watchdog Portman Group. Though for me it leaves a nasty taste in the mouth. Much as my own sensibilities are disturbed, one has to admire a brand that goes for the opposite of vanilla (and really goes for it, rather than lamely being a bit "edgy"). There is nothing faint-hearted about ramming your premium beer up a surprised-looking squirrel's bum, looking customers square in the eye and asking them to dig deep to pay for the privilege of drinking it.

Not quite as extreme (indeed, it strikes me as trying rather too hard) is North American brand Crystal Head vodka. Less a meditative memento mori, more a desperate shout for attention. The cod-nihilism might strike grown ups as a tad overcooked. But believe it or not, Crystal Head is as expensive as the (premium-positioned) Grey Goose and even more incredibly has accelerated from nought to $50m in sales in its first year. The bad taste might be more cheesy than provocative, but its success suggests there's a big market for innovation unencumbered by notions of nuance or 'authenticity'.

While both these brands could be seen as simply aiming to shock, they do at least use design to evoke something with an interestingly spiky persona. The dark side of life is little accessed by mainstream brands, but the sales of Crystal Head suggests it's a rich seam waiting to be mined. Imagine the same strategy executed with the subtlety and power of an old master painting. The memento mori has long been a powerful device in art and stands out brilliantly in a brand landscape that is usually happy and shiny – and it worked for the afformentioned Mr Hirst. Or perhaps such a meditative approach misses the point and would also miss the well-heeled pool of nihilistic rebels for which Crystal Head is presumably the vodka of choice? Whatever, there is certainly a market to be tapped where sustainability, sensitivity and progressive views are an anathema and the bad boys grab the glory. Which is actually quite refreshing.

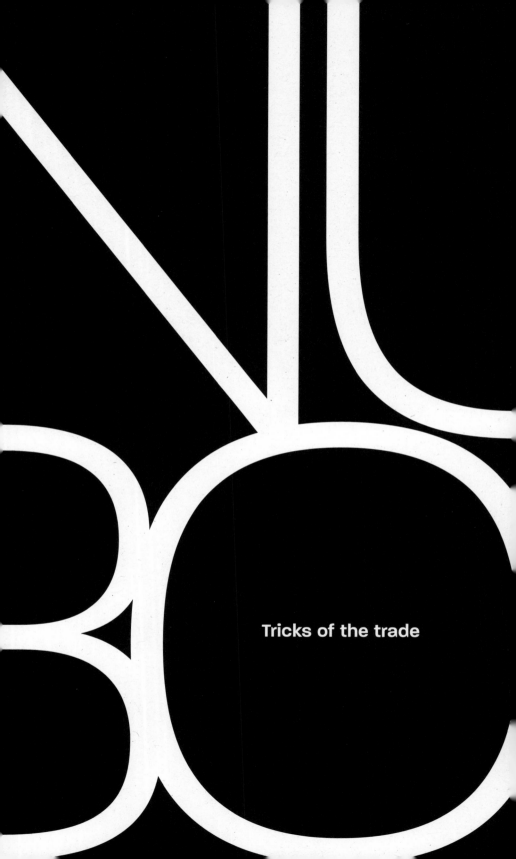

Tricks of the trade

The nuts and bolts of effective design are not necessarily complex. But like much in life, it's what you do with the same essential ingredients that is key. New solutions, that feel freshly minted, can be sparked by looking at what is in plain sight from a fresh perspective. What follows is a glance at some of the ways we are currently viewing design's kit of parts.

Ambition is only a matter of vision and ink

Communication comes in standard formats, to slot into standard displays, be it a cereal box in Tesco or a theatre poster in nineteenth century Paris. So how do some designs transcend the format and push their brand into the big time?

Aristide Bruant might be the father of shelf-blocking. He was just another chansonnier in a crowded market, but he obviously had an eye for design. It was he who insisted on having his poster for a residence at the Ambassadeurs theatre designed by the unknown Toulouse Lautrec. Lautrec stripped things to their essentials and played up the singer's dramatic red scarf. When the posters went up, the owner called them "pigwash" and ordered their removal. Bruant countered: "You leave it there. What's more, stick it up on the stage on both sides. And if it's not done by quarter-to-eight – eight's no good – I'll chuck in my number and disappear."[31] Framed by his image, Bruant's performance was an overwhelming success. The poster went up all over Paris, making his name and that of the poster designer. Bruant is my candidate for patron saint of fantastic clients.

Now, keeping things simple and striking might sound obvious. That such an approach lends itself to fantastic results when shown in multiples, equally obvious. But sometimes the obvious is easy to forget. The new design for Coco Pops might not be hanging in the Louvre in a century, but it has benefited from following this approach. While the old design was okay, its evenly balanced arrangement of key elements did not add up to the power of the new one because nothing in particular stood out. The redesign focuses wholeheartedly on the monkey and so catches the eye brilliantly when blocked on shelf. The chimp might be no chansonnier, but a simple design gives him the room to be the star.

The graphics that go on standard posters and packs are only a matter of the same ink in different arrangements. Yet it's possible to think big and convey a sense of grand ambition and heroic charisma that's compelling in itself. In graphic expression, even the smallest brand is on a level playing field with Coke. Just because you don't have their budget, it doesn't mean you can't match their graphic confidence.

Quick	Tardy
Cheap	Pricey
Good	Poor

As the old adage goes, clients can pick only two from the left column. If you want the job good and quick, it's going to be pricey. Cheap and quick, its going to be poor, etc. I guess the inverse equation works for agencies choosing from the right column.

Efficient design is overrated and craft is undervalued

"A good concept has to have a payoff in direct proportion to the time invested in creating it." This comment was posted airily on the *Creative Review* forum. It suggests that design and thinking should be elegantly economical, but the results should be powerful. But does this view place efficiency ahead of true creativity, thereby compromising the product and reducing the expected payoff? If you invest the proper time, the results can last down the centuries. The only trouble is, it's hard to see at the time if all that hard work is going to pay off.

Perhaps the comment says more about our lowering threshold for endeavour and craft and our rising appetite for quick results and fast turnover of design. Look at the sketchbooks of any of the design greats and you'll see that they fiddled away at versions of the potential solution for ages. Too much time on their hands? Or a desire to find exactly the right answer, rather than the "right now" one? As our world accelerates, the challenge for clients and designers will be to allow enough time for noodling. Long-term solutions rarely fall out of short-term deadlines. When time is tight, creatives often fall back on their experience and back-catalogue. Not a place one typically finds an appropriate and effective answer that is also truly original.

As we become addicted to instant results, fast-track cues and everything right-now, the training of creativity is being compressed and potentially compromised. One college promises to take folk with no experience from zero to a professional portfolio and in-depth knowledge of relevant programmes in just three months. Perhaps they can deliver, but I still believe our profession demands and deserves, more than a crash course. In pre-computer days, the technical challenges of producing slick visuals were daunting, but working at pencil speed did allow time to think and learn on the job.

Picasso was once asked to knock out a quick sketch on a chat show. Having obliged he was asked how he could justify the huge fee that his few seconds' work would command. To paraphrase his response: "It didn't take seconds, it took a lifetime."

Keeping on keeping on - it's half the battle

Evian has been putting out a New Year limited edition for years. Some are classics, such as 2005's glass mountain. Most have a celeb angle with contributions from designers such as Christian Lacroix, Jean Paul Gaultier, Paul Smith and Issey Miyake. This isn't short-term brand promotion: it's regular-as-clockwork brand behaviour and because it adds a new brick each year, it can be truly seen as brand building. Any individual pack might not be earth-shattering, but the cumulative effect is impressive. As the editions have a consistent fashion theme, the brand manager hardly needs to break sweat.

Evian isn't alone in having the commitment to stick with (but keep adding to) a good idea. BMW has been giving cars to fine artists to decorate whenever the spirit has moved them for years. Kleenex made a functional product fun with great seasonal packs that looked like slices of watermelon and similar messy things. Not resting on their laurels, they followed up with winter ones which decorated the box with the kind of box covers nanna used to knit to hide tissues back in the day. Either version released alone would be a slightly random spike of activity.

One of our clients is Molton Brown. Together we realised that if their ranges were bundled in "gift wrapped" packaging in the run-up to Christmas, then the packaging became part of the gift, saved stressed men having to wrap it up and also acting as in-store display materials. All good, but Molton Brown also challenge us each year to produce a new, better variation on the theme. Each year sales rise. It's a pressure to keep topping the previous year's edition, but also a great problem to have. This, essentially, is a design programme, not a design promotion.

By building on a coherent theme and having the energy to keep going and not getting lazy, such brands benefit from activity that's greater than the sum of its parts. Ironically, this approach offers a funnel of activity which is far easier to maintain than having no stamina, then finding oneself starting from scratch over and over again.

Design by word of mouth

Hitchcock called them McGuffins: plot devices that act as catalysts for a story, but are not as important to the plot as they appear. The briefcase whose contents are never revealed, but which nevertheless causes all the trouble in *Pulp Fiction*, is a classic McGuffin. Creative ideas can work like McGuffins, firing consumers' imaginations before the designer's pen has even been put to paper.

Can the Kellogg's laser make smoke without fire? A press release suggested they might use a laser to brand its logo onto individual flakes to mark them as superior to cheaper supermarket 'fake flakes'. Yet while this PR release quickly caught the imaginations of broadsheets, tabloids and bloggers, it had, in fact, only been one of many notions proposed by the food technologists, not yet even costed or trialled. Nevertheless, the idea was arresting enough to generate acres of free publicity.[32] Here, of course, is the substance of the PR coup. In a year when Kellogg's ran a big campaign around Henry Kellogg's signature and the message "If it's not Kellogg's on the box, it's not Kellogg's in the box", this helped drive that message home brilliantly. Would consumers want to look into a bowl of logos? Would this not undermine the famously natural credentials of the product? While this design proposal remained at the planning stage, such questions could also stay on the drawing board.

Similarly the plans to launch a chain of "Cadbury's Cocoa Houses" also gained lots of press, despite only being at the proposal stage.[33] This is in large part attributable to the mooted idea to sell XXL versions of Cadbury's famous products – it's the kind of thing which captures our imagination. "They're going to make big slices of Crunchie cake!" a colleague cheerily informed me, almost licking her lips. I think she had pretty much invented this detail in her own head, but that's the point. Fantastical ideas engage us and fire our imaginations without requiring the time-consuming and expensive research and development phase which would make them a reality. The XXL detail was the killer tweak that made this brand extension sing in her mind's eye: conceptual design without the use of a pencil.

Brandgym creator David Taylor talks compellingly of marketing's need to provide a good sausage along with the alluring sizzle. These stories prove that a neat idea, tactically deployed, can generate lots of sizzle before the sausage even exists. It might not be a sustainable approach, but it's an efficient way to generate free engagement with the brand.

Do we need celebrity designers?

By 'celebrity' I don't mean Lady Gaga's appointment as creative director of Polaroid. I'm thinking of those 'name' designers who develop a signature style: the Starks, Newsons and Carsons of our world.

Take Fabien Baron, inductee of the Art Directors Hall of Fame and subject of numerous broadsheet profiles. A great art director, he has added his stamp to famous publications (*Harpers Bazaar* and *Vogue,* perfumes, sunglasses, Madonna's *Sex* book and suchlike) for decades. When you hire Baron, you hire his style. But having a recognisable look runs counter to one view of what makes a great designer. This view suggests that designers should be chameleons, able to conjure up whatever style the job demands and focused on making the work famous, not the creator. As Luca Stoppini told the *New York Times* when explaining why she dismissed Baron from Italian *Vogue:* "With Fabien's design there was an overall sense of sameness, from article to article and issue to issue, which is his strength, even his gift, but just not my preference."[34]

Perhaps, but we need a few more Fabien Barons. Firstly, because brands often enjoy great leaps forward through design authorship: Neville Brody at *The Face,* Jonathan Ive at Apple. Secondly, with design's role taken increasingly seriously within marketing departments, marketing is becoming more populated with clients who see design as functional and serious business (with designers as functionaries). They feel qualified to meddle aesthetically. Clients with misplaced confidence in their own abilities as designers and a lack of respect for the skill of the people they have employed, can lead to the solution being okay but not great.

It's nothing new. There is a story that when (celeb-designer) Michelangelo presented his sculpture of David to Florence, one dignitary suggested the nose was a tad large. Michelangelo duly climbed his ladder and pretended to make corrections. Tapping with hammer and chisel, he sprinkled some dust from his pocket onto the crowd below. On the artist's descent, the dignitary proclaimed himself pleased with the results.

Against a trend that takes design very seriously while dismissing designers, the Barons and Ives of our age offer a reminder that sometimes you buy the vision and the talent – and should cherish it. Guys like them save the rest of us from being perceived as jobbing plumbers. We might not need gimmicky celebrity design appointments, but we will always need talented designers whose output has star quality.

UMBRELLAS

HAZELWOOD
HOUSE

EST.D 1830

SOLE MAKERS
of THE CELEBRATED
UNLIFFE SPORTS SEAT

James Smith & Sons

IFE PRESERVERS
AGGER CANES,
WORDSTICKS.

JAMES SMITH & SON
WHIP MAKER

James Smith & Sons
Established 1830

The power of slow

In Pompeii the surviving walls of a fish sauce manufacturer's home are decorated with mosaics featuring bottles of produce and proclamations of their fine qualities.[35] Moving forward 2,000 years, a recent film documenting the painting of a giant Stella advertisement on a New York wall gained plenty of attention, partly because investing in branding which has a physical permanence is now so rare as to be novel. The project chimes with a mini-trend in websites celebrating the 'ghost signs' of Victorian and Edwardian advertising, those faded echoes of the once beautifully elaborate painted advertising that graced the shops, pubs and eateries of our forebears' cities.

Why should investing time and craft in branding be a dying art? Why can a preserver of rotting fish entrails from the first century AD still have a promotion running, while it's a struggle to remember most press ads from last year?

Perhaps permanence went hand in hand with the time and effort it took to get the stuff up there. Filmmaker Don Letts noted in *The Observer:* "The downside of affordable technology is mediocrity. Back in the 70s every three minutes of film cost £20. Now you can get a 90-minute digital tape for a fiver. The price used to weed out the people who were fucking about."[36] Could a similar comparison be made in the difference between paint and pixels?

Or perhaps today's transient mentality is rooted within the "results now" culture of contemporary marketing. Brand managers are encouraged to be tactical and are under pressure to leave a mark before they move onto the next brand – and rung of the career ladder. Suggest an idea that could do the brand a lot of good but has little to do with this quarter's strategy and challenges and watch it roll into the long grass.

Yet maintaining long-term brand health makes good brands great. Might household names be better served by some kind of separate legacy fund – targeting the next fifty years, rather than the next five. Serving what's right for the brand long-term rather than what's right for right now? If 5% of a year's resource is devoted to new ventures, couldn't an equal amount be invested in visionary works, behaviour and branding that might feed the brand forever? Once the only limitation for beautifully rendered messaging appeared to be how high the sign painter's ladder reached. Do we, today's mainstream commercial artists, lack some of that vision and ambition in our expedient times?

Opposite: "They don't make 'em like that anymore!" (part two)

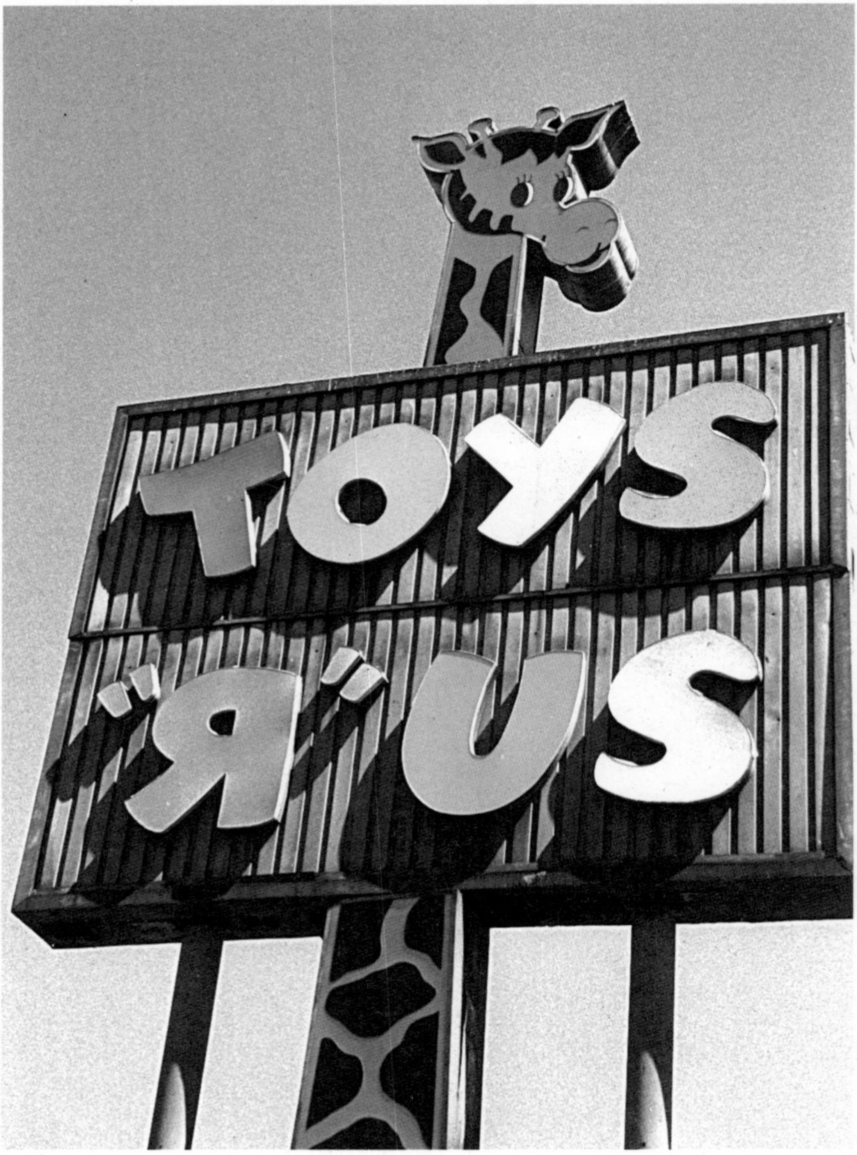

Image courtesy of Todd Franklin, Flickr

It's as much about what you remove as what you add

Lucky Strike Silver changed from the old red bullseye to a low tar category-relevant blue one. More generic maybe, but the detail impressed. The simple but visually nuanced vignette passing through the blue shows that subtly can have great impact. You can admire the brand's long loyalty to its red icon and its belief that variants could be managed through the name. However the new design drains none of the brand's power, yet is a darn site clearer if one is looking for a "lights" variant.

In pure design terms the pack architecture is a classic and colour change was key to its iconic status. Legend has it that designer Raymond Loewy told the client he could double the pack's impact *and* save them money. He achieved this by the simple measure of removing the green ink leaving a bright white canvas. This was also seen as a patriotic gesture, saving materials for WW2. Little things can make a big difference, which takes me back to the observation about the vignette.

Simplicity through reduction is a straightforward way to draw out and amplify any brand's true equities. Any decent brand manager will attempt to "add value", to deliver a pack with "more bangs for the buck". Typically, this will involve adding pack claims, or design detail that brings more appetite appeal or whatever. But as architect Ludwig Mies van der Rohe had it, "less is more". For every element added, the prudent brand manager should aim to remove something. Otherwise you risk saying everything, but telling the consumer nothing. Consider the iPod: against a trend for mp3 players where functionality was seen as the key indicator of quality and competitors were locked in an arms race to add more and more buttons, this design had one simple wheel. It was the purity of the design that stood out and was, truly, iconic.

Gunther Kilsheimer was another who understood the art of reduction. He was integral to the production of perhaps the most famous branding in toy retail. Kilsheimer designed a sign for "Children's Supermart Toys". Along with a new image, the client wanted a more upscale sign, one with individual 'channel' letters. When Gunther explained the cost of having so many letters in this style, the client asked for a name change. The result was *Toys 'R' Us*. But the 'R' had to be backwards, as if a child had written it. It's a good example of pragmatic thinking begetting a creative solution[37] and of a savvy client. In our straitened times, cutting back can actually deliver more, not less, if you're smart enough to spot the opportunity.

Pack shots are a golden opportunity, not a necessary evil

"Do we really have to put the pack shot on the end-frame?" bleated the head of planning at the ad agency, wrinkling her nose. The ad wasn't even written, but she was worried it would lose all its grooviness if it included something as old-fashioned and drearily commercial as an image of the product the ad was selling.

There are indeed lots (and lots) of really uninspiring and dreary pack shots in ads. Blame the art directors.

At their best pack shots can be the answer not the end-frame, with 'the brand in the hand' putting itself at the centre of its own story. In the early nineties, BBH brilliantly adopted the bold yellow and black iconography we designed for the Boddingtons draught can to create a seamless union of pack, brand and concept over a range of fantastic press ads. There's no doubt this made a huge contribution to making the brand both famous and refreshingly aspirational in a rather fusty world of drinkers who enjoy a pint of bitter. It won some coveted D&ADs into the bargain, proving that if you have imagination even something as old-fashioned as presenting your wares can be a creative exercise.

Of course, there are degrees. Cadbury's Gorilla would have been plonky with a bolted-on pack shot. But Gorilla still made use of the packaging's signature purple as a background, to deliver a strongly branded ad.

In a Christmas edition of one fashion magazine groaning with generic pack shot-heavy advertising for seemingly interchangeable designer jewellery, Tiffany's approach stood out. Having taken the trouble to build a distinctive brand, Tiffany can now show just the box not the product. In the image, a man stands head bowed on a doorstop, the box tightly gripped behind his back. He's psyching himself up to pop the question, in an image as rich in emotion and story as any Norman Rockwell painting. In the overall layout the pack was tiny, but due to its distinctive design, it remained the image's crucial storytelling element. The onus is on advertising creatives to work out how to use the packs creatively. It's the responsibility of the packaging designers to deliver work that has strong enough equities to inspire the ad guys.

Opposite: A campaign for Heinz Ketchup put the pack at the centre of the imagery and even changed the actual pack for a short while. If the iconography is strong enough it can support such tactical messaging.

"ASTONISH ME!!"

Rise of the machines

At last – a designer who doesn't need any sleep, food or stroking. Software from BETC Euro RSCG generates advertising. Give it data on brand, target, insight and strategic objectives and it spits out basic treatments. Offended creative directors tend to attack the results on sight. But "after this first reaction, they get a little scared when they see that a software program can create the same (mediocre) results in just 10 seconds as several hours of strategic meetings and production"[38] the RSCG executive creative director said. The programme is being positioned as a visualisation tool, used to illustrate the creative process rather than something which will steal creatives' jobs. But they've also got a development plan to keep improving the software.

Why wait to implement the prototype? Many clients are happier talking strategy and insights than dabbling in design. They'll greenlight dull work if it researches well against mediocre criteria. So why not let them use this software, freeing up the real creatives' to work with creative clients? I'd welcome software that tackled the donkey work in packaging design, such as global language conversions and outer shippers. It would free up creative budgets for creative endeavour.

Software designers can be a bit random when it comes to serving our industry. I used the £1.19 Brand Generator app to see if it could beat the number one packaged drink in the UK on-trade – J20. I gave Brand Generator the word "juice" to work on. It suggested Juiceeo, Eojuice, Juiceia, Lajuice, Juiceoos, Oosjuice. We gave the name Party Feet to a Scholl's gel arch support for high heels. What would the app make of the root word "party"? Partyeo, Eoparty, Partyia, Laparty, Partyoos, Oosparty. I think that's worth £1.19.

Software might miss the mark sometimes, but the real problem today is a generation of client trained to value insight over inspiration – always. Design without strategy is like advertising without a message. But design without ideas will never make a real difference. Strategically and creatively, programmed approaches can only ever ape, at best, the average in the market. Alexey Brodovitch, art director of *Harpers Bazaar,* famously instructed new recruits to "astonish me". Tell that to a computer.

feature presentation

the blue lady's new look

or why everything's looking familiar
...and how to make the most of it

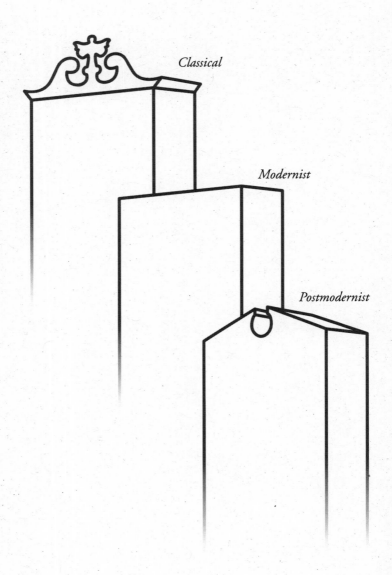

Classical

Modernist

Postmodernist

Vladimir Tretchikoff painted *Chinese Girl,* better known as *The Blue Lady,* in 1952. It was a massive hit, shifting half a million prints (supposedly outselling copies of The Mona Lisa). Its ubiquitous presence on suburban walls of the 60s and 70s made it a kitsch classic. The image adorning this book's cover is a recent pastiche of Tretchikoff's original. I first encountered this version in a Sunday broadsheet's style section, where it was set amongst similarly groovy modern-day designer lifestyle accessories. It stuck me as an emblem of design's current position. The new version is at once slickly contemporary, knowing and stylish, faux-vintage frame and all. It plays on our collective cultural knowledge, cannibalising and reworking a symbol from the past to appeal to contemporary tastes. It reflects our mainstream postmodern self-referential times. Our times are unique in the way they offer a blip in the hitherto relentlessly progressive trajectory of design.

The distinctive platter of artifacts that artists and designers produce visually defines each generation. Previously each successive generation's creative output built on or challenged the preceding era. So the florid curves of art nouveau straightened into the soaring lines of art deco. The necessarily stripped-down aesthetic of the utility era was countered in the flamboyant celebration of materials heralded by Dior's *New Look.* Each era had a particular flavour, easily labelled in hindsight. But today we dine on broth. Lovely broth, with choice ingredients wittily juxtaposed to tickle our palate. Broth in limitless varieties. But, nonetheless, broth: a rich blend of references and styles that offers us everything we have ever known, served up in a bowl, all together, all in one sitting.

Stephen Bayley, writing in *Intelligent Life* about minimalism, noted artist Grayson Perry's impression of the Basel art fair: "everything is happening now all at once".[39] Bayley continues: "There was no longer a ruling style or taste, no common agreement on what is avant-garde and what is retro-grade. Today the happening thing is just what is happening. We have reached the end of 'isms'." There is no one particular 'new style' or progressive single style by which we will be remembered. Rather, as we become more visually literate and attuned to the references around us, the defining sensibility of our times is an eclectic reworking of everything that brought us to this point. In design terms, time's arrow is spinning around like a weathervane in a hurricane.

The purpose of this closing chapter is not to bemoan the current lack of progressive spirit or to compare our times to previous eras and find us wanting. Rather it is intended to observe the current landscape, identify some reasons why it seems to be a breathing space between great leaps forward and to offer examples of brands and designs which are smartly reacting to the current state of affairs.

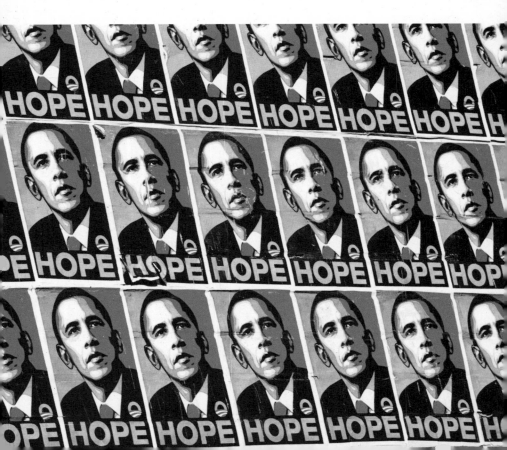

First, let's define our terms. I'm describing our era as *mainstream postmodern*. This label is increasingly used, albeit loosely. Simply put, it feels like much around us is familiar and it seems to me that even twenty years ago there were definite progressive styles in graphics and suchlike which I would struggle to put my finger on today. But what is *postmodernism* and where did it come from?

Before postmodernism came, logically, *modernism*. As the name suggests, it was progressive. A school of thought emerged in the early twentieth century that design featuring elaborate ornament and flourish was elitist. Decoration that was not integral to an object's function added cost and so put it beyond the pocket of the less affluent. Stripping things back to their essentials and exploiting modern industrial processes, cut costs and was therefore the 'moral' way to approach design. A Bauhaus chair, using developments in bent tubular steel, was a perfect early realisation of the approach.

To cut a long (and much disputed) story short, in the 1980s postmodernism took over the contemporary technologies and straightforward style of modernism but restored elements of design ornament, making wittily knowing 'tip of the hat' references to designs past.

The AT&T building (now the Sony building) completed in 1984 was immediately controversial for its neo-Georgian pediment which references Thomas Chippendale's wardrobes. Michael Graves' kettle for Alessi, in contemporary chrome, but topped off with a little bird stopper, was the Chippendale building's in-home equivalent. These designs were 'thought leader' rather than mainstream. 1980s postmodernism operated in a rarefied atmosphere of 'statement' architecture and designer knick-knacks coveted by art directors dressed in black polo necks. But while the term postmodern still has the ring of irrelevant academia, the template (knowing references, plundering the past and offering up stylistic juxtapositions and collages) has become the mainstream norm. Whether you believe postmodernism expresses a change in sensibilities or imposes one, it's the environment we all inhabit.

All those mainstream 'retro' and 'vintage' rebrands? Postmodernism without the fancy labelling. A pre-faded t-shirt emblazoned with the old Monster Munch logo, or Andy Warhol promoting Dom Pérignon in advertising and packaging from beyond the grave herald the mainstreaming of the movement. We can film our family moments on an iPhone, then convert them via Vintage Video to a grainy Super 8 effect, complete with scratches, jerky movements and the whir of a non-existent projector. Obama's famous *Hope* poster was essentially a pastiche of campaign imagery from the Kennedy era, with a nod to social realist art and a pinch of Che Guevara myth-making in the eyes-towards-the-horizon pose. A skilful weaving of many reference points and associations, the image tapped the optimism of earlier generations and was a significant factor in his election.

Referential design has great power because it co-opts values symbolised by designs of previous eras. Like a cross-selling suggestion on Amazon, it says "If you liked that you'll probably enjoy this."

Lady Gaga is the poster girl of mainstream postmodern celebrity. *Time* magazine included her in its 2010 Time 100 list of the most influential people in the world and *Forbes* listed her fourth on its list of the 100 Most Powerful and Influential celebrities in the world. Yet her image is constructed from famous ingredients of other acts: a pinch of Madonna's conical bra phase, a dash of Bowie's lightning-strike make-up, a side-order of Grace Jones' avant-garde fashion styling. It's served up as something new and it's massively successful. In an interview with *The Word* magazine musician Ben Folds praised her talent but described her oeuvre as "boneless". That's as pithy a definition of postmodernism as I've come across.

What's driving this boneless age? The economic downturn was widely credited with inspiring brands to remind us of their long pasts. Vintage advertising was recycled to re-establish brands' heritages and to celebrate their anniversaries. In times of worry, the theory went, we all go running to the comforting apron strings of brands we first consumed at mummy's knee. Fairy Liquid played to this when it reissued its "classic" white bottle. Familiar to a generation who followed Blue Peter's guidance on how to convert it into myriad craft projects. Fairy's follow-up advertising pastiched old ads from simpler times, as if to say "you might not trust the banks, but you can rely on us". Many other brands played the same game, reissuing archive advertising and heritage packaging to celebrate brand anniversaries. It was no coincidence that the poster of the moment was a reprint of an old Home Office piece of propaganda: "Keep calm and carry on."

But the real driver of our current obsession with referential design is, no surprise, the internet. The real leaps forward right now are in design's response to technology's disruptive challenges. Style, for now, is taking a back seat. The situation echoes the Victorian industrial age, when a romantic movement celebrating classicism and craft counterbalanced mass production's fundamental assault on established lifestyles. The steam age saw designers running for medieval Gothic styling. Our silicon age sees something similar.

I think there are three forces at work here. Firstly, as technology and communications evolve at a mind-blowing pace, we are all struggling to keep up with the basics. Crowds cheered when teenager Jake Lee bought the UK's first iPad and Rupert Murdoch called the device "game-changing". It isn't just newspapers under threat, but every communication rule we ever thought we knew. The medium really is the message and new platforms demand new design solutions. Is it any wonder that we grasp at familiarity, when the 'shock of the new' is a constant occurrence?

Secondly, the internet offers a bank of visual information ripe for designers to plunder which simply did not exist twenty years ago. Back then there were a few design resource books that could be found in every agency library. These gave helpful but brief synopses of past design styles and landmark moments. Now, if you're curious about, say, the commercial branding of VW vans in Europe in the 1950s, there are hundreds of examples instantly available. The detail is mindboggling – but it's made the big picture harder to see.

Thirdly, the wealth of new work and new thinking available on the web has made it harder to identify who the real leaders are. Design movements are made up of individuals clustering around a few leaders, borrowing and building a style that defines an era and adds something to culture. Who can keep up with the endless stream of thought leadership from the stage of TED, or the lists of 'must-know' influential designers? Abundance has blunted our ability to take design to the next leap forward. A tsunami of daily posted trend information has left us more rudderless (and uniformly dressed) than in the analogue era of, say, punk.

So, from the president to Lady Gaga, from crisps to champagne and from the Basel art fair to *The Blue Lady* print, we live in culturally self-referential and mix 'n' match times.

Which brands are smartly riding this wave? Simply put, there are two ways to react: to be wholeheartedly nostalgic or to use the best of the past as one ingredient in designs which also look to the future. Monster Munch and the retro Fairy Liquid pack take the former approach. Both have been successful, but theirs is not a long-term strategy. Nostalgia quickly outstays its welcome: "Nice to see you back. Yes we had some good times. Look, I'll call you again soon." Mixing old and new has a better chance of retaining relevance and building brands for tomorrow. It's trickier to look, Janus-like, in two directions at once, but the combination of hindsight and foresight makes for a more rounded and engaging approach than just putting on yesteryear's clothes. For want of a better term, let's call this strategy *retro-progressive*. (The phrase isn't original to me – but hey, that's postmodernism.)

The first set of examples use their visual equities (the signifiers of their tried and trusted values) but apply a new coat of paint. The redesign of Coke Classic is a textbook example of a great design that reconfigures equities, succeeding in polishing the brand's heritage in a way that appeals to contemporary tastes. Essentially, the can had become cluttered. The white wave line had sprouted go-faster stripes and other colours. There was a trompe l'oeil of graphic water droplets and so on. Moira Cullen, Coke's brand director, said[40] "We had to bring forward what was true about the brand… to make the complex clear – in the category simplicity was not the standard – not screaming and shouting benefits was a *very modern idea.*" (My italics.)

VMSEVE

The simplified design stripped back the identity to a look familiar to anyone who drank Coke in the seventies. Sounds simple, but in a marketing culture where adding bits and bobs to the pack is seen to add value, this can't have been an easy sell. The new design allowed Coke Classic to act once again as an uncluttered symbol for the refreshment inside the can, rather than trying to represent this promise literally. The can itself might be classical, retro even, but it acted as a catalyst for genuinely modern expressions of the brand, all sharing the same pared-back identity. So aluminium bottles combined the bold graphics with a bottle profile reflecting the famous glass design. Summer was celebrated on can with simple sunny icons like flip-flops and beach balls. It wasn't just the simplicity which was modern: Coke drew on its past to create new expressions. This respect for heritage filtered through contemporary graphic styling elevates the design above the one-note approach of 'retro' packaging, bringing new energy and relevance to the brand.

Kellogg's has similarly drawn down on an old equity to make a contemporary point. The company has made much of its founder's signature which endorses all its brands. A part of the brand's graphic armoury has thus acquired new emphasis as a guarantee of quality. This is particularly important in an era when value is everything and private label rivals are nipping at brands' heels to persuade mums that they are the smarter buy.

Virgin Atlantic's Red Hot campaign of 2009 dramatised the first appearance of its comely stewardesses in a retro eighties setting. The styling and message might have been nostalgic, but the objectification and cinematography were bang up to date. In the companion online imagery the stewardesses were photographed in a moody 'modern luxury' style that referenced contemporary style magazines like *Wallpaper**, all retro trappings dispensed with. While the brands noseart-inspired logo showing a flying girl in a red bathing suit owed much to the forties styling of pin-up artists such as Vargas. The spacesuit-wearing version used to herald the Virgin Galactic venture was a fantastic mix of the old with the very, very new.

Aston Martin owes much of its place as a leading creator of objects of desire to the classic silver DB5 which Sean Connery drove in *Thunderball*. All those kids with the Dinky toy model grew up, became big in the city and wanted the real deal. Obviously the brand is all about performance and this is the main feature of its communication – not too much time can be indulged wallowing in the past. Nevertheless, alongside Aston Martin's claims for the new V8's performance, the marque takes time to note online that the car is "modern, yet incorporating classic Aston Martin design cues". The shape of the car's grille is almost identical to Bond's and of course the car photographed is silver. Reconfigured equities authenticate the new expression by offering a glance back over the shoulder. Do it well, as Aston Martin does and you get to the number one position on the Coolbrand list.

All of these are examples of established brands that rework and visually amplify past glories to project their futures. The neatest example I can think of for this approach comes from Gucci, which has recycled sixties advertising for the brand. The ads feature black and white images of legendary model Veruschka as a backdrop for new watches branded with a contemporary translucent application of the Gucci logo. Gucci's creative director Frida Giannini explained that the archive shots "perfectly illustrate not only the glamour of Gucci's past... but also show how this heritage can be relevant today".[41] Of course the fact that the ads are selling timepieces makes the time-travelling dimension all the more pertinent.

This brings us to a second retro-progressive approach: inventing nostalgia. Giannini is also responsible for Gucci by Gucci, a new fragrance launched in 2007 whose design was effectively a hybrid of every equity Gucci had to muster. Recalling the brand's design heritage and evoking the spirit of Gucci in its seventies disco pomp. It distilled the essence of Gucci from old wordmarks, shapes, materials, the belt of stripes and the hanging horse bit. Giannini was said to have been attempting to create the perfume equivalent of the Nike flagship store, filled with the brand's past glories and devices. As the *New York Times* commented: "Gucci by Gucci winks at the memory of Sophia Loren's breasts busting out of a black silk dress in 1964."[42] The accompanying advertising compounded this message, with a Jerry Hall lookalike dancing around to Blondie.

Whether it's a case of new wine in an old bottle or vice versa, it's the combination of tradition and modernity that makes such branding 'pop'. While many brands used their birthdays to trot out old packs and TV ads, Selfridges marked its 100th anniversary by collaborating with famous brands and designers to rebrand famous products like Johnny Walker in the simple, stylish yellow and black of the store's identity. They also produced one-off new products such as Marc Jacobs's bags and Giles Deacon leather dresses, again in the brand's striking colours. This was a celebration of the past aimed squarely at the fashion forward's purse.

A recent example of invented nostalgia comes in the teaser campaign for *Toy Story 3*. Long before the film was released, fantastically convincing vintage ads popped up on the internet selling a craze from yesteryear – Lots-O'-Huggin Bear. They featured authentic looking .degradation from the original video and there was even a Japanese version. Plenty of the online comments came from people who fondly remembered the toy. But Lotso was a character invented for the movie, a kind of Care Bear with issues. Of course, after the film's release fact mirrored fiction, with the toy becoming available to buy for real. Agent Provocateur repackages such vintage sensibilities to create an aspirational and contemporary brand. After all, what could be more anachronistic than a corset? But with edgy advertising and a focus on modern day mores, the brand takes typography and structures from the era of 50s glamour and uses them to build a new superbrand from scratch.

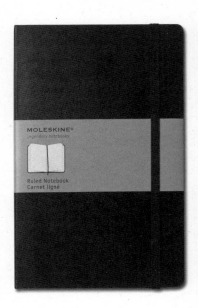

The Dita Von Teese packaging for Perrier featured elsewhere in this book also uses a rather old-fashioned expression of glamour to good contemporary effect, by applying the imagery to chrome cans with graphics that are decidedly 'noughties'. iPhone covers in Cath Kidston prints or Modo and Modo's relaunch of Moleskine notebooks (based on a classic design produced by several manufacturers, but marketed as "the legendary notebook of Hemingway, Picasso and Chatwin" creating a definitive 'original' from various sources[43]) are other examples of newly invented brands for today's world which nevertheless trade off our knowledge and affection for the past.

But the very best retro-progressive design is effectively a cladding for bold new technologies or progressive thinking. Perhaps one of the neatest examples comes from the Fiat 500 relaunch. While it follows the conventional formula of taking a well-loved classic car design and reworking it for contemporary tastes, under the hood the design offers real technological 'new news'. Start&Stop is innovative new technology developed in collaboration with Bosch and aimed at reducing fuel consumption and CO_2 emissions. As the vehicle draws to a halt at a junction, traffic lights or queue, the engine cuts out quietly while all other functions (indicators, heating, brake lights, sound system and electric windows) continue to operate normally.[44] This requires a sophisticated battery and other engineering breakthroughs, to ensure there's no jolting and juddering restart when the throttle is depressed. Drivers can also download and monitor their own eco-performance with information about the way the car is being driven added to a data stick plugged into a USB port inside the car. The data can be analysed alongside other drivers' data to offer tips to improve performance. Here we see a real hybrid of hindsight and foresight, with the fashion statement styling of a cute and curvy little car underpinned by genuine progress for the brand and the driver.

Similarly, the Quaker Oats US campaign "Go Humans Go" looks both old and new and offers up a progressive philosophy for the brand. Its traditional portrait of the brand's mascot against an iPod-white backdrop with typography that could be advertising a new app was an arresting juxtaposition of the traditional and the contemporary. But it wasn't just the art direction that added a contemporary feel to a classic look. "Go Humans Go" could be read as a progressive cheer to consumers struggling with the recession or a simple product claim, extolling the "good start to the day" credentials of the product. But it also nodded to the traditional humanist values of Quakerism. Either way, it was a cheerleader chant for tomorrow. Contrast this clever mixture of old and new with the brand's UK initiative, where we simply got a rehash of a historic pack artwork. The latter told us the brand had roots. The former told us Quaker had a vision. By looking in both directions, "Go Humans Go" was the more inspiring solution.

As this book surveys current design trends, I have avoided citing examples of design from jkr, the agency where I work, for fear of appearing self-serving. But I would like to round off by giving three examples of work we have produced recently which fit with my retro-progressive line, to demonstrate that there is some practice to go with the theory.

Hovis was a much-loved bread brand with sales in steep decline. Rival Warburtons was stealing share with packaging that evoked a traditional family baker. Hovis found itself perceived as "dry brown bread" (previous owners had cut corners to cut costs) and it needed to get its mojo back. The packaging was big on logo, but short on personality, despite the brand's proud history going back over a hundred years. The new Marketing Director did not have much time to spare and gave us a remarkably focused brief: "Reconnect us with what made us special. I'll fix the product, you fix the packaging." We went to the archive and reintroduced a wordmark and loaf device from the original advertising. We added a date and small illustration of "the boy on the bike": the character who had advertised the product in the classic Ridley Scott ad from the seventies. So far, so nostalgic. To this we added two contemporary twists: a bold contemporary colour palette and a distinctive pack architecture that took the previously fully enclosed design and made half of it a clear window. The bold colours helped consumers to navigate in-store through a wide range of products, while also delivering great standout. The clear window told shoppers that this was a fresh loaf the baker was proud to display. The design acted as a catalyst to the advertising brief, which featured the boy on the bike running through Britain's last hundred years of history, fetching up as a modern young lad in a contemporary kitchen. Sales pulled out of the spin and returned to growth. Reframing the past with contemporary styling gave the brand a future.

Penhaligon's is a classic British fragrance brand that combines a sense of quality with a quintessentially English eccentricity. We were tasked to design the Christmas packaging to a theme of "animals in outfits", which isn't a brief you take every day. At first glance the packaging has all the Victorian reserve of a long established and traditional brand: rich colours, cameo illustration in ornate frames, velvet ribbons and hatbox-like structures. But closer inspection reveals a bestiary of weird and wonderful creatures tricked out in their most elegant outfits. So the spirit of Lewis Carroll meets a classic brand in a design at once terribly proper, but also quietly contemporary.

Finally, the redesign of the Guinness can. As the brand celebrated its 250th year, we were given a fantastic brief: "Make the Guinness can great, not good." For, while the pint of Guinness in the pub was a thing of beauty and distinction, the can was a poor cover version in comparison, using a vignette of silver to evoke the product's famous "settle and surge" but falling short of being an icon in its own right. This was an issue as sales increasingly moved from the pub to at-home consumption.

For a brand which needs to retain relevance for younger men, Guinness had a challenge on its hands. Our design simplified things, going for a single-minded black can with a strong use of the brand's traditional harp logo. This created a more powerful badge in the hand and also evoked the confidence of a brand that had always carried itself in a powerfully charismatic "less is more" manner. Again sales went up. But, just as importantly, the new design, which represented traditional elements in a contemporary manner, acted as trigger for further resolving the brand's overall identity. Informing the creation of templates for product photography, typography and suchlike and so helping to build a more unified and distinctive evocation of the brand as a whole.

These three examples share a common design philosophy: that the strongest brands have at their hearts simple and boldly presented symbols. Given the visual literacy of today's consumers and their ability to decode graphic symbolism, this is an approach not exclusive to revamped brands. Any symbol we encounter on shelf instantly triggers a wealth of associations in our heads about the brand, its history and our experiences with it. Or at least it does if the designer has done their job and created a pack which is distinctive and idiosyncratic. But the more established the brand, the richer the bank of associations waiting to be triggered. As with the Obama *Hope* example, some of this is down to our ability to read design as code and some of it simply to do with recognition. But many great brands are returning to purer expressions of their core symbols, the better to make the trigger work. The fancy name for this is "involuntary memory", but it's more commonly known as the Proustian rush – that moment when a smell, an image or sound suddenly transports us to another time and place (hopefully for the brand a happy and engaging one). It is the opposite of deliberately recalled memory because it just happens, in a fraction of a second. The best retro-progressive branding delivers a walloping Proustian rush while also offering up a style or content which feels either timeless or contemporary.

But is the use of past designs to inform a vision for the future enough? Are we, as the representatives of an era, selling our times short? Such questions suggest that we have a choice to do otherwise and I don't believe this is the case. Commercial art is a reflection of where we are culturally. Where we are offers plenty of scope for play and endeavour. Ian Rickson directed the contemporary play *Jerusalem*, a big hit and is now at work on his hotly anticipated production of *Hamlet*. As he told *The Guardian:* "The challenge is to make a text that can be so familiar feel urgent and resonant and fresh. I like the idea of treating classics as if they are new plays and new plays as if they are classics."[45] Which is quite an inspiring perspective on the opportunity.

As noted in this book's technology section, new media tend to beget new forms of visual communication. I think we're simply catching our breath.

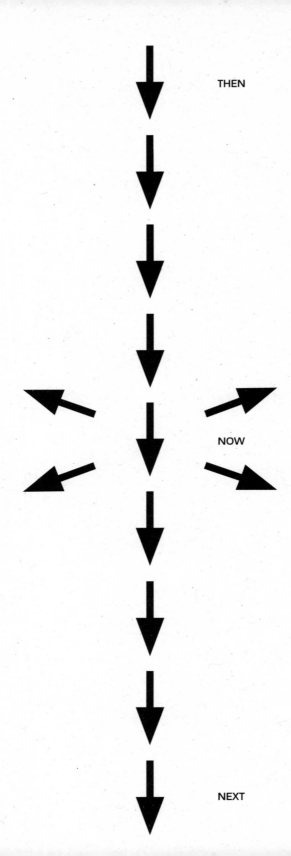

THEN

NOW

NEXT

Let's take a moment to enjoy the scenery, because pretty soon we will be plunging on, creating and consuming design that is right now just a spark in the eye of some junior graduate sat in the corner of an agency or marketing department. Here's to the future and to work the like of which we've never seen before... At which point it will be "goodbye to all that".

appendix & acknowledgements

WARNING
This article contains unsourced, unverified information from Wikipedia.

The stickers on this page were designed by Tom Scott. They were intended to be cut out and stuck to any media which the reader perceived to be lazy or biased journalism. The book in your hands is a prime candidate for such stickering – it has built up daily as a blog (not a medium noted for its academic rigour). Nevertheless I have endeavoured to keep track of my factual source material and offer this up for anyone who wants to read further.

WARNING
This article is based on an unverified, anonymous tipoff.

WARNING
This article is basically just a press release, copied and pasted.

WARNING
Statistics, survey results and/or equations in this article were sponsored by a PR company.

1. In Wolfe's clothing, John Freeman. 18 December 2004. *The Sydney Morning Herald* (via Wikipedia).

2. Tory MP tables Bill to scale down 'hardcore' lingerie posters on London's buses. Wednesday 10 March 2010. *Evening Standard.*

3. Dove's Men+Care to target the silver foxes, Alex Beckett. 09 January 2010. *The Grocer.*

4. *Subaru Gets Serious About Design.* 14 July 2010. Pistonheads.

5. CBR, Paradise Highlands, Martin Grey. 20 January 2010.

6. Wordswarm.net

7. Ever Heard of The Trogon? RJ Evans. 14 March 2010. Scienceray.com

8. The virtual reality stats were pulled from *The Observer* newspaper, in summer 2010. The article does not appear to be saved on the Guardian site.

9. Augmented reality: it's like real life, but better, Charles Arthur. 21 March 2010. *The Observer.*

10. Artificial meat? Food for thought by 2050, John Vidal. Monday 16 August 2010. *The Guardian*

11. Rupert Murdoch says Apple's iPad is a 'game-changer' for news media, Andrew Clark. Thursday 5 August 2010. *The Guardian.*

12. 100 Thoughts, HSBC Bank insert (76-100) in *The Times.* 2010.

13. Navigating Complexity: Doing more with less, 11-12 April 2007. Almaden Institute / IBM online.

14. @ at MoMA, Paola Antonelli. March 2010. Inside/Out. MoMA online.

15. Ferrari ditches controversial barcode livery, ESPNF1 Staff. 6 May 2010. en.espnf1.com

16. Peanuts Comic strip rights to be sold to iconix, 27 April 2010. Businessweek.com.

17. Red Goalkeeper tops help save penalties, The Goalkeeper.com.

18. *Go Faster: The Graphic Design of Racing Cars*, Sven VoelKer. 2010. Die Gestalten Verlag

19. Boris Johnson's London Cycle Hire scheme flogs our birthright to Barclays, Justin McGuirk. 27 July 2010. Guardian.co.uk.

20. 100 thoughts (25-50), HSBC Bank insert. 2010. Distributed with *The Times* newspaper.

21. This piece was original requested by and written for *Design Week* – used with permission.

22. The Toxic Side of Being, Literally, Green, Alice Rawsthron. 4 April 2010. *New York Times.*

23. Chanel muses on global cooling with iceberg show, Sophie Hardach and Mathilde Gardin. 9 March 2010. Reuters.

24. Deeper luxury, Jem Bendell and Anthony Kleanthous. Nov 2007. Report by the World Wildlife Fund.

25. Hershey's Packaging Perfectly Contradicts Itself, 7 December 2009. Agency Spy.

26. *Family Britain, 1951-1957 (Tales of a New Jerusalem),* Bloomsbury. David Kynaston. 2009.

27. Ethiopia firm recycling tyres into shoes does big business via internet, Xan Rice. 3rd January 2010. *The Guardian.*

28. UPS is driving more miles than ever, but using less fuel, Jeffrey Davis. 10 August 2010. Greenwala.

29. The Dell / bamboo story came from CBS News online. The original link has proven hard to trace.

30. Frankfurt showcar Audi e-tron, Press release. January 2010. Audi.co.uk.

31. *Toulouse Lautrec,* Gilles Neret. 2009. Taschen.

32. Kellogg's laser logo will fight against fake flakes, Miles Erwin. 14 October 2009. *Metro* newspaper.

33. First Cadbury Cocoa House to open in October, Rosie Baker. 25 August 2010. *Marketing Week.*

34. Fabien Baron: The Art Director as Star, Cathy Horyn. 26 September 2008. *New York Times.*

35. *Pompeii: The Life of a Roman Town,* Mary Beard. 2009. Profile Books.

36. This much I know: Don Letts, Gareth Grundy. 22 August 2010. *The Observer.*

37. Gunther Kilsheimer, Pioneer in Graphic Arts Passes Away at Age 86, Wednesday 12 August 2009. Press Release, Art Display Company.

38. Don't Tell the Creative Department, but Software Can Produce Ads, Too, Stuart Elliott. 27 August 2010. *The New York Times.*

39. Does Minimalism Matter? Stephen Bayley. Autumn 2010. *Intelligent Life.*

40. Entry Film, D&AD awards. 2009. Dandad.org

41. Gucci Flashback Ads, Feb 2010. rdujour.com

42. Scent Notes | Gucci by Gucci, Chandler Burr. 13 December 2000. *The New York Times Style magazine.*

43. *Phaidon Design Classics.* 2006. Phaidon Press Ltd

44. Fiat 500 Start-Stop review, Iain Robertson. 2009. WhatGreenCar.com

45. After Tony Blair and Brian Clough, Michael Sheen to play Hamlet, Charlotte Higgins. 13 May 2010. *The Guardian.*

Acknowledgments

A deep breath and feeling not unlike Gwyneth Paltrow clutching her Oscar, I have a large number of folk I wish to thank for their part in helping this book reach your hands. Amy Maw tirelessly gets the Design Gazette "up" online each day. It is the raw material of this book. For this, sourcing all of the book's imagery, herding cats, making the project happen and doing it all with a smile, I give her my heartfelt thanks. Paul May has again been a dedicated editor and again a great advisor. A friend in need is of course a pain in the proverbial, but two good friends of mine answered my plea for help – Neil Ireland and Steve Rigley had the unenviable task of ploughing through the book's first draft, helping me to order my random thoughts and pointing out many things I had missed. If you find errors or stupidity in these pages the faults are mine, but both Steve and Neil made an invaluable contribution to what ended up on the page. Rory Sutherland has my eternal gratitude for consenting to write the introduction, although it is slightly irritating being presented with copy that puts the rest of the book's writing so firmly in the shade.

Thanks Alex Stewart for co-designing the book and Nick Little for all the pack photography and retouching. A tip of the hat also to Hannah Roberts and Andrew David for their toils on the production and artwork roles respectively.

With copyright issues to be mindful of and a budget tighter than a gnat's chuff, we had to rely on the kindness of strangers. We were not disappointed. Folk approached through finding their work on Flickr generally turned out to be a hugely generous breed and I want to thank Jeanne Nguyen, Peter Nicholas Wood, Christopher Campbell, Olly Courtney, David Wilfert, Rebecca Campbell, Ali Muskett, Nick Turner, MOSO® Products, Todd Franklin, Thomas Hawk, Ken Brown, Ron Artigues and Rick McOmben for allowing us to use their work on pages 16, 52, 60, 68, 70, 74, 76, 86, 102, 120, 130, 132, 136 and 140 respectively.

Thanks also to Tom Gauld for granting permission to use his artwork on page 26. Thanks you to jkr staffers Chris Burge and Sean Lingwood for their illustrations (on pages 40, 44, 108 and 90, 114, 124 respectively) and Kuba Wieczorek for his fantastic photographs on pages 82 and 118. And for kicking off a train of thought and being gracious enough to allow her illustration to be used for our cover, many thanks to Miss Swanne.

Finally, thank you, reader, if you have made it this far!

Thank you for
reading. Please
feel free to recycle the
thinking, or even better,
pass this book on...

The paper in this book is accredited:

The jkr Design Gazette will continue to offer free thinking most working days in 2011. www.jkr.co.uk/design-gazette/ *

*or just google "jkr design" - it's quicker!